teach
yourself

flexible working
carol elston and
sue orrell

For over 60 years, more than
40 million people have learnt over
750 subjects the **teach yourself**
way, with impressive results.

be where you want to be
with **teach yourself**

For UK order enquiries: please contact Bookpoint Ltd, 130 Milton Park, Abingdon, Oxon OX14 4SB. Telephone: +44 (0) 1235 827720. Fax: +44 (0) 1235 400454. Lines are open 09.00–18.00, Monday to Saturday, with a 24-hour message answering service. Details about our titles and how to order are available at www.teachyourself.co.uk

For USA order enquiries: please contact McGraw-Hill Customer Services, PO Box 545, Blacklick, OH 43004-0545, USA. Telephone: 1-800-722-4726. Fax: 1-614-755-5645.

For Canada order enquiries: please contact McGraw-Hill Ryerson Ltd, 300 Water St, Whitby, Ontario L1N 9B6, Canada. Telephone: 905 430 5000. Fax: 905 430 5020.

Long renowned as the authoritative source for self-guided learning – with more than 40 million copies sold worldwide – the **teach yourself** series includes over 300 titles in the fields of languages, crafts, hobbies, business, computing and education.

British Library Cataloguing in Publication Data: a catalogue record for this title is available from the British Library.

Library of Congress Catalog Card Number: on file.

First published in UK 2005 by Hodder Education, 338 Euston Road, London, NW1 3BH.

First published in US 2005 by Contemporary Books, a Division of the McGraw-Hill Companies, 1 Prudential Plaza, 130 East Randolph Street, Chicago, IL 60601 USA.

The **teach yourself** name is a registered trade mark of Hodder Headline.

Typeset by Transet Limited, Coventry, England.
Printed in Great Britain for Hodder Education, a division of Hodder Headline, 338 Euston Road, London NW1 3BH, by Cox & Wyman Ltd, Reading, Berkshire.

Hodder Headline's policy is to use papers that are natural, renewable and recyclable products and made from wood grown in sustainable forests. The logging and manufacturing processes are expected to conform to the environmental regulations of the country of origin.

Impression number   10 9 8 7 6 5 4 3 2 1
Year   2010 2009 2008 2007 2006 2005

contents

acknowledgements

The authors and Publisher would like to thank the following for their kind permission to reproduce copyright material:

Arthur Allen (Listawood Ltd); Kelly Bennett (Royal Bank of Scotland); Gerard Bithell (BT); Sean Blessitt; Gill Brown; Sue Chand (Leeds Metropolitan University); Caroline Cheales (Surrey County Council); Heidi and Martin Cheek; Professor Shirley Dex; Michelle Duggan (Scottish Enterprise); Michael Fidler (Access Migration); Dawn France (HBOS); John Gelson (GNER); Nicole Gerrey (Moneypenny); Phil Glanfield (NHS); Maggie Graham; Ian Greenwood; Carol Hampson (Beardmore Conference Hotel); Robert Hawkins; Brian Holmes (EEF); Caroline Hopkins (East Riding of Yorkshire Council); Glyn House (Sainsburys Ltd); Sue Laycock; Sharon Love (NHS); Carol Mack (Surrey County Council); Angela Macleod (Work Global); Kerry Martin (Access Migration); Alan McAvan (HBOS); Donnie Morrison (Work Global); Dan Pankethman; Ryta Prentice; Martin Shelly (NHS); Jane Stapleford (Leeds Metropolitan University); Mark Taylor; Michelle Tennens (Red Pepper Marketing); Judith Wardell (Kingswood Consulting).

The publisher has used its best endeavours to ensure that the URLs for external websites referred to in this book are correct and active at the time of going to press. However, the publisher has no responsibility for the websites and can give no guarantee that a site will remain live or that the content is or will remain appropriate.

introduction

Work/life balance is the buzz phrase of the 21st century. Pick up any lifestyle magazine and you are likely to find an article telling you how you can achieve a better balance between your working life and personal commitments. The key seems to be flexible working, be it part-time, job share, working from home or one of the many other options available to workers today. By taking a flexible approach to work you can spend more time with your family, have more of that elusive 'me time' or simply work at a time that suits you, rather than the rigid '9 to 5' imposed by many organizations.

So, if flexible working has so many benefits why are less than a quarter of the employed population choosing this alternative? Finance can be a major stumbling block; dreaming of working fewer hours is one thing but unfortunately less hours usually means less pay. For others, there is no choice; some organizations do not offer a flexible working environment in any shape or form whereas others claim to have a flexible working policy but only pay lip service to the idea. Unless an organization is truly committed to flexible working, from the top down, the culture within the workforce can make it difficult for employees to take advantage of the options available.

Even for those organizations that are open to flexible working, there are still issues. The main barriers seem to be finding the time, resources and money to put the schemes into place. There are also major concerns regarding managing staff remotely. With home working for instance, managing workers from a distance creates new challenges. Managers need to adopt a new mindset, they need to learn to trust employees and judge performance on productivity rather than hours worked. In the office environment a manager can see, first-hand whether an employee is coping, struggling or capable of taking on more. In the case of remote working the manager has to find alternative methods for people management; monitoring performance, setting targets and organizing communication channels are just a few of the tasks that are essential to the smooth running of the operation. Methods of communication also need to change with email, video conferencing and the sharing of information via the Internet becoming second nature.

Employees also need to learn new skills when opting for a flexible working life. They need to work with their manager to determine how they will organize their workload within the constraints of the agreed working pattern. If job sharing they need to take responsibility for communicating with their partner and providing a seamless role to the organization. Home workers may have an even more daunting task, maintaining productivity, managing guilt, isolation and technical issues as well as making sure they remain part of the organization and are not over looked when it comes to promotions and training opportunities.

It may all sound rather gloomy, but many of these challenges and issues can be dealt with simply by changing the culture of an organization. Surveys show that the benefits of flexible working far outweigh any negative aspects, for both employee and employer. There are plenty of examples of employers that have been encouraging their staff to work flexibly for years with many more waking up to the benefits of a flexible workforce, nudged into action by recent legislation. As for the employee, the benefits are huge: less stress, more control, more time with family. The list is endless and what's more, flexibility doesn't always mean less pay. By maintaining the same number of hours but changing when you work, you can greatly improve the work/life balance.

So, with most employees appearing to welcome flexible working and statistics showing that work/life balance initiatives can save an employer a significant sum in recruitment and retention not to mention the huge savings in accommodation costs, flexible working has to be a serious option for the future. Without doubt, our productivity as a nation will suffer if we do not provide more working alternatives – roads are already clogged up with rush hour traffic, city centre parking and accommodation is at a premium and most importantly we do not have enough human resources to fill the ever-increasing skills gaps. By offering more working alternatives we can minimize downtime and attract skilled employees, such as the retired and full-time mothers, back into the workforce.

Taking all these challenges into consideration, this book aims to provide a detailed look at the current working options accessible to the UK workforce. The first few chapters consider the vast menu of flexible working options available looking at relevant legislation, employee rights and future developments. Further chapters discuss the option of working from a flexible location, either working from home or on the move, paying particular attention to the major advances in technology that have undoubtedly fuelled the move towards flexible working locations. Remaining chapters consider the skills and mindset required by both an organization and an individual to successfully operate flexible working.

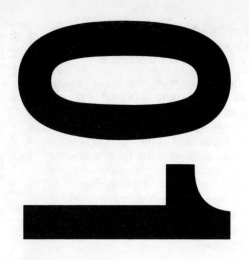

01

flexible working options

In this chapter you will learn:
- what flexible working is
- the benefits and issues of flexible working
- the types of flexible working options available
- the future of flexible working

What is flexible working?

The term flexible working is used to describe variations on the traditional '9 to 5' work model. Far from being a new phenomenon, workers in manufacturing and many service industries such as hotel and catering regularly work shifts outside the standard 9 to 5 day. Equally some progressive organizations have a long history of providing innovative schemes to achieve optimal use of their human resources as well as provide an improved life balance for their staff.

So, why is it that flexible working has suddenly become so newsworthy? There are a number of reasons:

- Advances in technology have made it possible to extend the options to office environments.
- Employees are being given more autonomy in finding a work pattern that is suitable for their personal situation.
- The Government is actively encouraging us to become a more flexible workforce through both legislation and marketing initiatives.

Without doubt, flexibility around when, where and how people work can benefit employer and employee alike. From an employer's perspective flexibility provides the opportunity to schedule working hours to meet the business's demands. From the employee's point of view flexibility can mean the freedom to organize work around family and personal commitments. Even the Government benefits from the initiatives. Flexible working can help with traffic congestion and reduce the demand for office properties.

The good thing is, flexible working doesn't suit one group more than another. There are plenty of people who are keen to work flexible hours especially if they have some choice when it comes to scheduling the days or shifts that they work. Equally, there are a growing number of enlightened employers who are realizing that flexibility will help them employ, retain and motivate quality staff. With communication and compromise employee and employer can often find a flexible working arrangement that suits them both.

Benefits and issues

The benefits and issues regarding flexible working are very much dependent on the situation and the individuals involved but, in general, they can be summarized as follows:

For the **employee** the major benefits include:

- improved work/life balance
- less stress and time commuting to work (home or remote working)
- more control over time off (compressed hours, term-time working, part-time working, job share)

and the major issues include:

- cut in pay (reduced hours)
- isolation (home working)
- lower status, lack of promotion opportunities (perceived or otherwise)
- difficulties communicating with colleagues and managers.

For the **employer** the major benefits include:

- managing fluctuations in demand
- providing extended cover (up to 24-hour)
- retaining valued staff who request flexibility
- making more efficient use of facilities and equipment

and the major issues involve:

- trust and supervision
- communication between staff working at varying times
- optimizing the use of buildings and facilities
- integrating part-time, non-permanent and home working staff
- achieving fairness in benefits for all staff.

Types of flexible working

The flexible options offered by an employer will depend on the type of business they are running. Most businesses are able to offer flexibility to some staff but there are roles that cannot be flexible due to the nature of the duties. To find out more about the types of industries offering flexible working see Chapter 2, Flexible working – is it for you?

In general flexible work options fall into three categories:

- flexible hours
- flexible contracts
- flexible location.

In addition there are flexible arrangements designed to accommodate lifestyle changes such as maternity and paternity leave, sabbaticals and retirement. These options can be grouped together under the category:

- flexible lifestyle options.

The following sections consider the most common flexible options available within each category, considering the advantages and issues for both employer and employee.

Flexible hours

Implementing an option of flexible hours invariably means providing alternatives to the standard 9 to 5, 5 days per week model. The most common options for non-standard or flexible hours arrangements are:

- flexi-time
- part-time working
- job sharing
- annualized hours
- compressed working hours
- shift work
- self-rostering
- staggered hours
- term-time working
- voluntary reduced working hours or V-Time
- time accounts/flexi-days.

Flexi-time

Flexi-time usually involves working a set of 'core hours', often 10 am until 3 or 4 pm, or at the times when an organization is at its busiest. Employees are expected to work the core hours but can vary the hours that they work either side of this. Alternatively, some businesses provide an even more flexible approach and require employees to work a specified number of hours, usually 7 or 8, during a 12-hour period such as 7 am to 7 pm. The degree of flexibility offered will depend on the type of business and the requirement for customer facing activities. Schemes that do not impose core hours need to rely on staff to ensure adequate cover during the working period.

The hours worked are sometimes recorded using time-management software although some organizations do still use punch cards or clocking in systems to register and track employee hours. More progressive organizations work on a basis of trust, expecting that employees will work the specified hours without being monitored.

Is it for me?

As an **employee**, would it improve your work/life balance if you could:

- avoid the rush-hour commuter traffic? ❑
- take or pick up the children from school? ❑
- start work late or leave work early in order to pursue a hobby or fitness routine? ❑
- have more flexibility to schedule personal appointments at either end of the day? ❑
- schedule quiet times at the start or end of the day to get on with work? ❑

As an **employer**, would it help your business prosper if you could:

- recruit and retain staff who have other life commitments or interests? ❑
- schedule work over a longer working day, so extending customer service? ❑

TIP: Flexi-time is certainly not favoured by all managers; poorly administered schemes can run the risk of becoming a free-for-all with staff turning up for work when they like. Some managers also fear the lack of control and prefer their team to work the same hours as they do. Such attitudes are fuelled by the assumption that people only work when supervised. For flexi-time to work successfully, managers need to trust their staff and monitor by output (or be prepared to put in very long hours).

Part-time working

Part-time working has always been an option for some but with the increasing demand for a better work/life balance more people are now considering it as an alternative. Since 1971 the number of part-time workers has increased from 2.2 million to more than 7 million with surveys consistently showing that the majority of people who work part-time do so because they want to, not because there is no choice.

The majority of part-time workers are women. However, with the growing emphasis on improving health and gaining a more balanced life, surveys show that an increasing number of employees of both sexes are considering working less hours. A recent European survey found that more than 54% of employees would like to work fewer hours. Gender does seem to make a difference to the motivation for seeking part-time work. For men, combining work with education or allowing more leisure time are the main reasons for wanting to work less hours, whereas for women, the main incentive is combining work with family responsibilities.

With so many people wanting to work part-time it is somewhat surprising that more workers don't reduce their hours. There appear to be four main reasons why they are reticent: economics, supply of quality part-time positions, entrenched attitudes and the perception that part-time work inhibits progression.

1 The inevitable cut in salary does make part-time work a non-viable option for many. Older workers in particular consider loss of income and a reduced pension a major obstacle in the take up of part-time opportunities.
2 Quality part-time positions are in low supply. There are certainly far fewer part-time jobs than people who would like them.
3 Part-time work is still thought of as being of lower status. Entrenched attitudes also associate part-time work with women's roles resulting in some men being reluctant to reduce their working hours.
4 There is also the view that part-time work inhibits both career progression and professional development and unfortunately this is still the case in less progressive organizations.

Legislation has yet to tackle all the disincentives of part-time working. The promotion of work/life balance initiatives has started to change attitudes but if the aim is to meet the European goals to attract more people into employment and create a more flexible workforce, attitudes will need to change further.

For the majority, part-time work improves the work/life balance but as Ria's story shows part-time working can bring its own stresses.

Case study: University HR Manager

Ria works as an HR Manager for a University in the Midlands. She started working part-time (31 hours a week) when her first child started school and has recently returned to a full-time position after four years of part-time work. Having experienced both situations she is now able to look back and compare the working arrangements.

'I was grateful for the opportunity to work part-time, I didn't want to stop working but I knew that I wanted to help my children settle into school life. We arranged it so that I worked 9.30 until 2.30, Monday to Wednesday and full days (9 until 5) on Thursday and Friday. That way I could take the boys to school and pick them up three days a week and only needed to arrange for an out of school club for two days.

'This arrangement met my objectives, but looking back I certainly paid a price. At times it was extremely stressful. I'd often arrive at work to find that an important meeting had been scheduled for 9 am and I had to join in, half an hour late. Also, meetings arranged for later in the day always seemed to run over which meant I was anxiously watching the clock and then dashing out at the last possible minute.

'If I had my time again I would still work part-time while the boys were young but life is much easier now that I am working full-time. The boys go to an out of school club every day and are quite happy with this and I have much less stress to cope with.'

Is it for me?

As an **employee,** would it improve your work/life balance if you could:

- have more time to pursue hobbies and non-work activities? ❏
- reduce the pressures of a full-time job? ❏
- have more time with your family? ❏

To achieve these objectives can you:

- manage on a lower income? ❏
- overcome any perceptions you may have regarding status?
- ensure that you uphold your rights for equality and career progression? ❏

As an **employer,** would it help your business prosper if you could:

- retain the skills and experience of (usually female) workers who want or need to reduce their working hours? ❏
- recruit quality staff who are only prepared to work part-time? ❏
- harvest the skills of part-time workers who are often more productive than their full-time equivalent? ❏

Job sharing

Job sharing usually involves two employees working on a part-time basis to cover the duties usually carried out by one full-time person. On occasion you may find that more than two people are involved in the job share but this is unusual as continuity becomes more difficult when more than two people are involved.

Both job-sharers receive pay for the hours that they work, usually based on a 50:50 split, but other variations are possible. Holidays and other benefits are divided according to the hours worked.

Good communication systems and skills are essential if a job share is going to work successfully. With some job share arrangements the employer will want both workers to have at least half a day in common so that a face-to-face handover can take place. Other job share roles can work well with a telephone or written handover to pass on necessary information regarding current tasks and issues.

Formal job share arrangements are still comparatively rare with less than 1% of the workforce choosing this flexible arrangement but they are becoming more common, particularly within the public sector.

Case study: Royal Bank of Scotland

Joan Cleft and Ruth Lambert both work for the Royal Bank of Scotland in the UK sharing the role of Personal Assistant to the Director of Retail Regulatory Risk.

It was Joan who initially suggested the job-share arrangement. Before her maternity leave she had worked full-time for the Director of Retail Regulatory Risk and was keen to return to this role, but on a part-time basis. Ruth was already working in the same department on a flexible contract that involved working alternate weeks. By working together the two women could fulfil the full-time role. They decided to opt for the alternate week arrangement as it suited Ruth's personal commitments and they also felt that it would allow them to minimize the handover by completing as many tasks as possible by Friday. They ensure continuity by producing a handover note that gives an update and details of any issues outstanding from the previous week.

From the business's point of view Joan and Ruth communicate well and respect each other's views and suggestions on work issues. Both women use their own time for medical and other personal appointments so that they can always work the full week without the need for time off. The Director of Retail Regulatory Risk is more than happy with this arrangement and confirms that no difficulties have arisen since the job share commenced over four years ago.

As for Joan and Ruth, they both agree that the arrangement means they can still have a career with the Bank but are also able to spend more time at home with their children and families; the best of both worlds.

However, for some, a job share arrangement may not work out quite so well.

Case study: National charity

Nadia works for a national charity; she works a job share with flexible hours and is based from home. Although this sounds like the ideal job, Nadia does have some reservations when it comes to the job share.

'If I were to apply to work another job share I would ask to meet my job share partner before accepting the post. This didn't happen with this job but if we had met I don't think I would have taken the job. The first few months were very difficult. Although the job share was at her request my partner obviously resented me and made it quite clear that she didn't appreciate any new ideas or suggestions. I stuck with it and tried to distance myself as much as possible and it has got better with time; we have now both learnt how to minimize conflict.'

The positive aspects of job share for both the employee and employer are similar to those of part-time work. However, as an employee there are some additional considerations to be made regarding your ability to work closely with a job share partner.

Is it for me?

As an **employee**, do you have the skills to:

- work in an organized way so that your job share partner can easily pick up where you finish? ❏
- understand the need for and use communication systems effectively? ❏
- communicate succinctly and efficiently with your job share? ❏

Annualized hours

Annualized hours is a flexible working scheme based on the number of hours worked during a year rather than a week. It is down to the employer and employees, often with the assistance of their trade union, to agree the total number of hours to be worked during the year. Schemes vary, but typically the annual hours are based on a 35- to 40-hour week multiplied by the number of weeks in the year less annual leave and public holidays.

This type of flexible working is most common in industries that have peaks and troughs in demand throughout the yearly cycle. The annual hours can be scheduled to match the levels of demand. This can reduce the need for overtime during busy periods and help to prevent employees being left idle during quieter periods. Although traditionally used by the manufacturing sector, annualized hours can suit any business with seasonal or periodical fluctuations in demand.

Scheduling of work can take a variety of forms depending on demand. In some cases there may be a period of intense work followed by 3-day weeks. In other organizations the fluctuations may be less extreme. Remuneration is often averaged out over the year so that the employee does not experience the variations in their salary payment. This can cause problems however if an employee leaves the organization part way through a year. When this does occur the pay due is calculated and the employee is either owed additional salary or is in the position of having to reimburse the organization for any amount they have been over paid.

This added complication can result in some employers adopting a 'pay as you go' annualized scheme. In this case the weekly or monthly pay reflects the hours worked. This method of payment is common with agriculture organizations where labourers' hours fluctuate depending on the time of year.

Companies operating within Europe are required to conform to the Working Time Regulations, which restricts an employee to working an average 48-hour week and defines minimum rest periods. At the moment, UK employees can choose to opt-out of the Working Time Regulations allowing them to agree to work more than an average 48 hours a week. There is a possibility that this opt-out clause may be phased out which could have drastic consequences for those organizations operating annualized hours schemes. For more information, see Chapter 3, Your rights as a flexible worker, The Working Time Regulations.

Annualized hours contracts have also caused concern for trade unions. Possibilities of exploitation, health and safety issues related to periods of intense working, and the erosion of overtime opportunities have all been seen as negative outcomes of the scheme. However, trade unions also appreciate that such arrangements can work well for employees with variations in the intensity of employment allowing them to pursue alternative activities during the quiet periods.

Case study: EEF Yorkshire and Humberside

Brian Holmes is employed as Head of Employee Relations for EEF Yorkshire and Humberside. EEF is the UK's largest industrial employers' organization providing a range of employment-related services for the 6,000 member companies. EEF Yorkshire and Humberside has over 400 member companies and it is Brian's role to help them achieve their business objectives.

Brian has recently helped a local printing firm manage a change to an annualized hours working arrangement.

'I was called in to help resolve differences. Basically Bob (the owner of the business) had no choice; profits were down and he had to do something. His business is fairly specialized, printing stationery for school and colleges, and over the last few years a definite pattern of demand had appeared. They were working flat out from January through to June and then had a much quieter period for the rest of the year. Schools tend to place the majority of their orders at the beginning of the year to use up budgets before April expecting delivery in time for the next school year, in September.

'Bob found that he needed to pay overtime during the busy period and sometimes even take on casual workers and then he had people sitting around with nothing to do later in the year. He came up with an annualized hours scheme, which meant that his employees would need to work longer hours during the busy period and have time off during the quieter months. It was my job to help him sell this to his staff.

'It was a battle; they were resistant to change but in time they started to see the benefits and understand that, as an organization, they had to change to survive. And now, two years down the line, I'd have a riot on my hands if I suggested they returned to their original working arrangements. I guess it's fortunate that they get time off during the summer months and the run up to Christmas, but I think it's true to say that they all prefer working annualized hours.'

It would be unusual for an individual to negotiate an annualized hours scheme with an employer. Such schemes are usually run for the entire organization or a department within the organization. If this type of flexibility appeals to you it is worth investigating opportunities within organizations already operating annualized schemes.

Is it for me?

As an **employee,** do you have the flexibility to:

* work long hours for some periods during the year? ❑
* have quieter periods when you are free to pursue other interests? ❑

As an **employer,** would it help your business prosper if you could:

* schedule employees to work longer hours during peak periods (without having to pay overtime rates)? ❑
* schedule employees to work fewer hours during quieter periods? ❑

Compressed working hours

Compressed working hours is becoming an increasingly popular option allowing employees to work their total number of agreed hours over a shorter period. Schemes vary but among the most common are the 4-day week and the 9-day fortnight. In the case of the 4-day week the employee works their total weekly hours in 4 days rather than 5. Although this results in longer working days the employee has the advantage of an additional day off every week. The 9-day fortnight works in a similar way with the employee having additional day off every fortnight.

With compressed hours schemes employees are paid for a full-time job and do not receive overtime payments for any extra hours they work in any one day. This can benefit the employer as they receive cover outside the standard working hours without having to pay overtime. Compressed hours schemes can only work successfully if the hours worked are scheduled sensibly. Although many workers would choose to tag their day off on to either end of the weekend not everyone can do this.

Case study: Surrey County Council

Employees at Surrey County Council in the UK have the option to compress their full-time working week into a 9-day fortnight or 4-day week. For both options, the non-worked day can be fixed or floating depending on the arrangement that suits the team or service. Start and finish times can also be fixed or flexible again depending on the team's needs.

Tony, Senior Planning Officer in Sustainable Development appreciated the flexibility that compressed working gave him when his son was younger.

'I opted for the compressed working time to help with my son's childcare. It was great to be given the opportunity to work flexibly, without having to reduce my hours, but it did put pressure on me to ensure that I was putting in the hours and getting the work done. Until I changed to compressed hours my workload, spread over 5 days, had not been a problem. Working just 4 days a week meant I could pick up my son from childcare and look after him on the fifth day, but my workload did need some extra juggling to make up time lost. Fortunately, because my wife is a teacher, I was able to work 5 days a week during the school holidays to catch up and meet my contractual requirements.

'Although I was extremely grateful for the ability to work so flexibly, I certainly found that it brought extra pressures with it.'

Is it for me?

As an **employee**:

- would it improve your work/life balance if you could regularly have a day off work in addition to the weekend without reducing your salary? ❏
- do you have the flexibility to work longer hours on the days that you are working (you will usually need to work an additional 7 to 8 hours over a 4-day period if you opt for a 4-day week)? ❏

As an **employer**, would it help your business prosper if you could:

- have cover outside of the standard working day without having to pay overtime? ❏

Shift work

Shift working provides scope for businesses to operate for longer periods than the standard 8-hour working day. Traditionally shift working was adopted by the manufacturing sector where it made economic sense to utilize plant and machinery for as many hours in the day as possible. With industries such as foundries, where it costs both time and money to get the furnaces set up and working, continuous use is the most commercially viable option.

Shift patterns vary; day and night shifts, week on week off, fortnight on fortnight off, and three-shift patterns are just some of the options. The traditional 6 to 2, 2 to 10 and 10 to 6 three-shift pattern provides for 24-hour cover. With this type of shift pattern the weekends are sometimes worked on an overtime basis or this period is used for maintenance of plant and machinery.

Public sector industries such as hospitals, the fire brigade and police force also need to provide 24-hour cover. Service sectors such as hospitality have traditionally provided out-of-hours service and many other employers are now realizing that longer opening hours can benefit their business as well as offering their employees more flexibility as a result of shift working.

In some cases shifts that fall within unsociable hours will attract premium rates of pay, traditionally time and a half for Saturday and double time for Sunday. However as the range of flexible working patterns has developed, agreed flexible working arrangements often mean that a shift premium is not paid as part of the deal; working 'unsociable' hours is accepted as being just an element of the job.

TIP: Shift swapping can be a formal or ad hoc system for enabling staff to negotiate their working times and shifts among themselves, while keeping the needs of the business or service in mind.

Case study: NHS and Fire Brigade

Heidi and Martin are both shift workers. Heidi works for the National Health Service (NHS) and Martin works for the Fire Brigade. With some clever planning and manoeuvring Martin and Heidi have created a working life that fits around their family. With two children of school age they have managed to coordinate their shifts so that they require minimal levels of external childcare and only occasionally need to call on friends or family.

Martin works annualized hours that equate to around 42 hours each week. He works 2 days from 9 am to 6 pm followed by 2 nights from 6 pm to 9 am. He then has 4 days off and the pattern starts again. This is an 8-day rota, the hours are set and Martin can work out his shifts a year in advance. This stability is crucial to the coordination of their shifts as Heidi's shifts are far more flexible.

Heidi works 22.5 hours a week, term time only. There is flexibility within those working hours and Heidi may work more hours one week and then less hours the next. In an average week Heidi works three shifts, either 7 am to 2.30 pm or 1.30 pm to 9 pm.

Heidi says, 'Our shifts at the hospital are scheduled a month in advance and because I know Martin's rota I request that I don't do a 1.30 pm to 9 pm shift when he is on nights. I can do the evening shift if Martin is on days; we use an after school club on an ad hoc basis so we have cover until 6 pm when Martin finishes.

Problems can arise if we are held up. Neither of us are in the kind of jobs where you can just down tools at the end of your shift and go home. If Martin is called out to a fire or accident of course he stays until it is sorted. In the same way, there are times when I can't leave a patient. For times like this we have a pool of friends that we call to look after the children.'

Martin says, 'When I am late I accrue overtime which can be useful. What I tend to do is use it to come home early from a night shift, around 6.30 am so that Heidi can do the 7 am to 2.30 pm shift. On the whole it works well, one or both of us always manages to attend school events and we usually have some time off together during the week while the children are at school. Our social life does suffer but at the moment the family comes first and the way we work is definitely the best fit.'

Is it for me?

As an **employee**, would it improve your work/life balance if you could:

- work hours other than the standard 9 to 5 (to fit in with partners, cover childcare, care for a dependant, allow for education)? ❑
- work unsociable hours to secure a higher rate of pay? ❑

As an **employer**, would it help your business prosper if you could:

- operate outside the standard 9 to 5 working day? ❑

Self-rostering

Self-rostering provides even greater flexibility for those working shifts. With this type of shift work the employer determines the number of staff required and the type of skills needed for each working period. The employees then put forward the times that they would like to work. Shift patterns are compiled matching staff preferences to the agreed staffing levels as closely as possible. Self-rostering is often used in hospitals and the care services and can work well if administered effectively.

Staggered hours

Some companies operate a system of staggered hours to ensure that they have staff available for longer than the standard 9 to 5 working day. With this type of arrangement employees have individual terms of conditions of employment detailing their start and finish times and in some cases their break times. In this way the employer has cover throughout the day with staggered lunch and break times.

Staggered hours are often adopted by the retail and hospitality sectors ensuring that there is sufficient staff available to cover the busy lunchtime period and less staff available at either end of the day when it is generally quieter.

This type of arrangement can be ideal for those employees with commitments at either end of the day. From the employer's point of view staggered hours provides cover for a longer period of time without the need to pay overtime. Employee pay is based on the number of hours worked regardless of the time they start and finish.

Is it for me?

As an **employee,** would it improve your work/life balance if you could:

- regularly start work later or finish work earlier?   ❏
- have set break and lunchtimes?   ❏

As an **employer,** would it help your business prosper if you could:

- operate outside the standard 9 to 5 working day without paying overtime?   ❏
- organize maximum cover during the busiest period if the day?   ❏

Term-time working

Term-time working enables parents and carers to take unpaid leave during school holiday periods. A term-time working contract will often be negotiated on an individual basis although some organizations do offer this option to all staff. In general the employee will specify the amount of unpaid leave needed, often in the region of 9 to 10 weeks. Added to paid annual holiday entitlement this works out at around 13 weeks, the average school holiday period for state schools.

The advantage of this type of scheme is obvious but there are drawbacks for both employee and employer. The reduction in salary is possibly the most apparent issue for the employee but there may also be problems of continuity and the risk that their role may be undermined during their absence. These obstacles can be managed if there is a good working relationship between the employee, their manager and the third party covering the role.

From the employer's point of view this type of flexibility may only be acceptable as a strategy for retaining staff. Although they will be saving on salary, long periods of leave can be disruptive and productivity or service can suffer. However, on occasion term-time working can benefit everyone as this case study from the NHS shows.

Case study: NHS

One Teaching Hospital in the UK came up with the novel idea of running a term-time only ward. The hospital had advertised for a team to staff the urology ward but had little response. In desperation they took the unprecedented decision to only open the ward Monday to Friday, to day patients and only book patients in during term time. The ward was a huge success – patients that had been on the waiting list now had a dedicated ward and nursing staff with commitments outside of work could join the workforce and utilize their skills. The majority of staff were responsible for childcare but not all. One member of the team was married to a teacher and liked to take off and travel the world during the summer holidays.

Unfortunately the project was short lived. After a year the ward was merged with a full-time ward as part of an NHS restructuring, much to the disappointment of the team who had benefited from this unique arrangement. The original team are still employed on a term-time only contract but have been moved to other wards within the hospital.

Is it for me?

As an **employee**, would it improve your work/life balance if you could:

- take unpaid leave during school holiday periods?   ❏

and do you have the flexibility to:

- take a reduction in salary?   ❏
- manage the psychological and practical implications of taking time off?   ❏

As an **employer**, would it help your business prosper if you could:

- employ and retain quality staff who have family obligations?   ❏

Voluntary reduced working hours, or V-Time

Voluntary reduced working hours, or V-Time, is a scheme by which permanent employees can agree with their employer to temporarily reduce the number of contractual hours that they work for a specified period.

This type of flexible arrangement is negotiated on an individual basis and is usually requested as a result of a personal or domestic difficulty that will be resolved in time.

For example, an employee may decide to make an application to their employer to work V-Time due to bereavement or a temporary breakdown of childcare arrangements.

Time accounts/flexi-days

Time accounts or flexi-days are formal methods for taking time off to compensate for extra time worked. In many ways a time account scheme is a more flexible form of the compressed working week or even annualized hours, with the employee having more control over when they take time off.

This type of scheme can be abused with staff working additional, non-productive hours simply to accrue time in lieu. However, if administered efficiently both employer and employee can benefit with staff putting in the hours when and if they are needed to be compensated by taking time off at a later date.

To work successfully there need to be some rules otherwise employees can find that they have unmanageable credits. It is usual to specify the maximum number of credits allowed preventing build up of holiday time or excessive periods of working. In some cases there is also a time limit in place for using the credits. Some companies incorporate other employee benefits and initiatives into the scheme by offering credits in place of other incentives such as bonuses or insurances. It has even been known for a company with a Green Travel Plan to offer time credits to those who do not drive to work.

Flexible contracts

Organizations are always looking for ways to improve their market responsiveness, by keeping costs down at the same time as maintaining quality. For many the solution is flexible contracts. By employing staff on a flexible contract basis they can manage periods of high demand without incurring long-term costs.

Contract workers

Contract workers are usually self-employed or employed by an agency that finds them suitable work. Before looking at the types of flexible contracts it is worth considering the workers that suit this type of working arrangement. In general there are three groups of contract worker although it is always difficult to categorize individuals. For the purposes of this section, the groups will be discussed as follows:

- portfolio worker (contractor)
- temporary worker (temp)
- freelancer.

Portfolio worker

A portfolio worker can be loosely defined as a self-employed individual who has managed an assortment of jobs on a contractual basis at various stages in their working lives. This recently devised label is usually reserved for skilled professionals who can demand high rates of pay and often work on specialist projects. A contractor is an alternative title for this type of flexible worker, certainly within the IT industry. Portfolio workers or contractors often have different objectives to temporary workers. Portfolio workers consider their roles to form part of their career often being selective regarding the contracts accepted. They tend to have an overall vision and are working to develop and increase their skills. Temporary workers often look at a contract as a stopgap, a way of earning money between jobs or other pursuits.

Organizations are learning to appreciate the benefits of employing qualified professionals as and when required. This flexible approach prevents the need to increase the permanent headcount in times of economic uncertainty. However, staffing costs can be increased due to the higher rates demanded by some portfolio workers. It is a case of balancing the risks – whether to employ permanent or contract staff is often a difficult decision.

Portfolio workers are often project-based; being brought in for the duration of the project or specific task. Some organizations have also found that including portfolio workers in the staffing mix can have the additional advantage of energizing permanent employees. The portfolio worker adds a spark of creativity, which can benefit everyone.

Portfolio workers need to be highly motivated and be able to cope with a working life that brings emotional and financial uncertainties. Many choose this lifestyle to improve their work/life balance but it can be stressful with periods of either feast or famine. A portfolio worker's financial situation has to be able to cope with this. On a more positive note, this type of work brings fresh challenges, the chance to meet new people and is often financially rewarding.

To be a successful portfolio worker follow these four simple steps:

• Have a business plan; know where you are going and what you want to achieve.
• Research your market; find out where the jobs are and what skills are in demand.
• Make sure that you have the right skills; training and development is your responsibility.
• Network as often as you can; you are your own marketing department, talk to people and listen, opportunities arise in the most unexpected places.

Is it for me?

Portfolio workers are a special breed and it is not a working life that suits all. Consider your experience, skills and temperament. If you are able to answer yes to the majority of the following questions it may be just the role for you.

	Yes	No
• Are you highly motivated?	❏	❏
• Are you able to strike out on your own?	❏	❏
• Do you have self-discipline?	❏	❏
• Are you a good time-manager?	❏	❏
• Can you work independently?	❏	❏
• Can you cope with emotional uncertainty?	❏	❏
• Can you cope with financial insecurity?	❏	❏
• Do you have cash reserves to ride out a start-up period and any periods of famine?	❏	❏
• Are you able to organize flexible financial arrangements?	❏	❏
• Are you focused enough to turn down unsuitable contracts?	❏	❏

Temporary worker

A temporary worker, often referred to as a temp, can be defined as someone who works for an organization on a temporary basis rather than as a permanent employee. Temporary contracts can differ in length from an hour to months or even years. Temporary workers can be employed to cover for permanent staff who are sick, on holiday or on maternity leave or they can be required to provide additional cover during busy periods.

People opt for the life of a temp for many different reasons. For some it is the variety that is appealing, the change of scenery, new people to meet and new challenges. For others it is the flexibility that attracts them, with temporary contracts providing the opportunity to fit work around other commitments. But for many a temporary contract is a means to an end, a stopgap between permanent work or a method of earning money during university holiday periods.

Temporary contracts are also a good way to try out a job without the commitment of a permanent role from either side. Many temps stay on in temporary roles for longer than first anticipated and organizations will often snap up quality temporary staff if they are prepared to work on a permanent basis.

Is it for me?

Working as a temp can be liberating or incredibly stressful, depending on your personality and outlook on life. If you answer yes to the majority of the following questions it may be the ideal working life for you.

	Yes	No
• Do you thrive on new experiences?	❏	❏
• Are you a friendly and open person that can easily fit into a new environment?	❏	❏
• Are you quick to learn and not afraid to ask questions?	❏	❏
• Are you adaptable?	❏	❏
• Can you manage financially if you have periods without work?	❏	❏
• Do you enjoy being in control of when you work and when you don't?	❏	❏
• Is your flexibility more important to you than career development?	❏	❏

Freelancer

A freelancer is usually a self-employed worker who is home-based and often works for several employers at the same time. This of course is a generalization and there are plenty of exceptions to the rule. In fact, it is a fine line that differentiates the portfolio worker, freelancer and temp and many flexible contractors fall into more than one category during a given working year.

A freelancer may identify with either the portfolio worker or the temp, depending on their motivation and reasons for working freelance. For some it is a way of gaining experience and widening their skills, for others it is a way to earn money and keep their hand in while pursuing other life goals.

The life of a freelancer combines well with parenthood, particularly those roles that can be home based such as freelance writing and journalism. Freelancers often work for several employers on a mutually flexible basis. This type of flexible contact can be formally defined as a zero hours contract (see later in this chapter) where the employer is under no obligation to provide work and the worker is equally under no obligation to accept work.

Case study: Robert Hawkins

Robert Hawkins has been a freelancer since August 1993, much longer than he initially anticipated.

'I'd just finished college and had written some freelance motoring articles as a student. I didn't need much money to survive, so considered the risk of freelancing would be better to take then instead of later in life when I may have a mortgage and children to support.'

At that time there were various schemes in place to help the self-employed.

'I consulted the Prince's Youth Business Trust (PYBT) and a business start up service in Hull to see if it was viable to start my own business as a journalist and photographer and decided to give it a go. With a £1,500 loan I bought a laptop computer, borrowed my Dad's cameras and started as a full-time freelancer. A business start up scheme paid me a weekly wage for six months, which helped to pay the rent. A business adviser from the PYBT met me on a monthly basis to discuss the progress of my business.'

Since those early days Robert has built up a large client base, working as a journalist, author and IT instructor.

'Over the years I've worked for three different IT agencies and about 20 magazines. I currently work for CATS Consulting as an Instructor as well as ten different magazines writing computer and motoring articles.'

When asked about the pros and cons of being a freelancer, Robert listed the following:

Pros:

- better pay than a staff writer/photographer
- if organized, good holidays (8–10 weeks per year)
- expenses are tax deductible
- freelance market is very healthy at the moment.

Cons:

- expansion is limited
- bad debts with new magazines are difficult to resolve
- some magazines drop you without notice
- long-term income is limited
- legal copyright on words and photos is in the hands of the magazines.

'As a freelancer I can be vulnerable, I was owed £600 by a classic car parts supplier for writing catalogue articles, who went bankrupt and promptly started up again owing nothing. And as to copyright, they decide the rules. IPC have world rights to my photos so I cannot sell them elsewhere. VNU buy 100% rights to my articles and subsequently publish them in other magazines and books without any additional payment to me.'

Now with a wife, son and mortgage, Robert is still freelancing. Does he intend to get a 'proper' job?

'Not yet, however I'm constantly watching the freelance market. Despite that it's less hassle for magazines to buy freelance work, it's much cheaper to employ a staff writer who can produce articles. One of my main customers, a computer magazine is moving in this direction and often writes all their features in house. They are also using articles written in other countries and translating or re-writing them. I certainly can't afford to be complacent.'

Is it for me?

Freelancers need to be highly motivated as contracts can be short lived and they always have to be in pursuit of the next assignment. On the other hand, this type of role is the ultimate in flexibility. If you answer yes to most of the following questions freelancing may suit your lifestyle.

	Yes	No
• Are you highly motivated and disciplined?	❏	❏
• Do you have the confidence to sell yourself?	❏	❏
• Are you focused and good at managing your time?	❏	❏
• Are your private commitments unpredictable?	❏	❏
• Do you need flexibility to manage other commitments?	❏	❏
• Can you manage on a flexible income?	❏	❏

Types of flexible contract

The most common flexible contract arrangements are:

- fixed-term contract
- temporary contract
- zero hours contracts.

Fixed-term contract

A fixed-term contract requires the worker and the employer to agree a term of engagement. The length of the term will usually depend on the reason for the contract being available. Organizations offer fixed contracts for many reasons including cover for an employee taking maternity leave or a sabbatical or for the duration of a specific project.

As a result of legislation introduced in 2002, workers who are engaged on this type of flexible contract are 'entitled to no less favourable terms and conditions of employment than an employee, including any special benefits'.

Fixed-term contracts can be renewable but there are rules in place to prevent an employer from using consecutive fixed-term contracts to avoid paying employee National Insurance contributions. For further information on the rights of a fixed-term contractor, see Chapter 3, Your rights as a flexible worker.

Temporary contract

The majority of temporary contracts are arranged by agencies. Take the common scenario:

* employee calls in sick;
* employer telephones an agency and requests a temporary worker to cover for the rest of the week;
* the agency searches its database for suitable workers who are available;
* they phone a worker and arrange for them to cover for the sick employee.

Other temporary contracts may be advertised in local papers or through job centres. In general the contract will be for a limited period with rates of pay quoted by the hour or week.

Workers securing contracts through an agency are employed by the agency and not the organization that they go to work for. If an organization recruits the temporary worker direct, however, they are considered to be the employer.

Traditionally, temporary workers have received lower rates of pay and less benefits than a permanent employee. Many view this as a fair arrangement, as the employer is acquiring the temporary services of someone who may not have experience of the role or understand the culture of the organization, making them less productive than their permanent equivalent. Equally, the temporary worker may accept a lower wage as they have the advantage of flexibility and they do not have the responsibilities of their permanent equivalent.

However, this is not the way it is viewed by all and a new European Directive is designed to protect the interests of the temporary worker by introducing legislation to ensure they have equal conditions of employment to permanent employees. From an agency and employer perspective this is not welcome news.

At the time of writing the proposals are beings discussed. At this stage the UK government agrees with the principle of protecting the rights of temporary workers, but feels that the minimum wage and working time directive have gone a long way to achieving this. Chapter 3 provides further information on the rights of the temporary worker and the anticipated effect that the new directive will have if and when it is adopted.

Zero hours contracts

A zero hours arrangement is effectively an on call arrangement where the employer requests the worker to work certain hours or days and the worker, in turn, either agrees or refuses. The relationship between the employer and worker is usually without obligation; the employer is not obliged to provide work and the worker is not obliged to carry out any work offered by the employer.

An employer who operates in this way will usually have a pool of workers that they can call on when work is available. Some employers will offer a retainer to maintain the services of workers, which could be a minimum level of work over a specified period of time. Alternatively employers may offer an incentive to ensure workers' loyalty such as training, the use of facilities or discounts on goods or services.

Agencies for temporary workers often work on this kind of basis, as do organizations requiring specialist skills on an ad hoc basis. This type of flexible contract often suits freelance workers who usually work for several organizations at the same time. By entering into such a mutually flexible arrangement they are able to refuse work when they have other commitments.

Case study: CATS Consulting

Change Associated Training Solutions (CATS), is a training and development company based in North Leeds. Although zero hours contract is not a term that they are familiar with this is exactly how CATS operates its business. Up until a few years ago CATS employed a number of permanent instructors providing training courses for clients covering both IT and soft skill applications. More recently they have changed the way they operate. The range of courses they offer is diverse and there was no way that their team of permanent trainers could cover all the topics. They found that they needed to employ freelance specialists to teach courses on an ever-increasing basis. Eventually they have reached the position where the majority of their teaching staff are freelance specialists that they call upon when needed.

The Directors of CATS Consulting Ltd are delighted with this arrangement. Staff costs have decreased as staff are only employed when needed, customers are happy as the pool of instructors can cover a vast range of topics and the freelancers are able to enjoy a flexible lifestyle.

Flexible location

The last decade has seen huge advancements in the technologies that have enabled employees to work from locations other than the traditional workplace. With the development of laptop computers, mobile phones and wireless technologies it is now possible to work from almost anywhere. As so many people are now looking to work from a more flexible location this book dedicates two chapters to this option. Chapter 4 considers working from home with Chapter 9 looking at the options available for working on the move.

Flexible work/life choices

There may be a time during your working life when you decide to take a break from being an employee. You may choose to become self-employed or take time away from working completely either to pursue another interest or care for dependants. This section looks at a range of flexible work/life choices that can be taken during a working life:

- self-employment
- retirement
- sabbaticals
- maternity/paternity leave.

Self-employment

Self-employment provides flexibility in many forms. A self-employed person can be an employer, a portfolio worker, a freelancer, a home worker; the possibilities are endless. The subject of self-employment is a book in its own right but it is not an area we have chosen to cover as a 'stand-alone' topic. Instead, we have incorporated information and advice for the self-employed within every chapter.

Retirement

The State Pensionable Age is currently 60 for women and 65 for men in the UK. Traditionally the working life ends on a specified day, the day of retirement. For some this clear-cut conclusion is desirable whereas others may prefer to retire early or take a more gentle approach, phasing in retirement more slowly. But for a number of employees, the retirement day holds dread and they are anxious to prolong their working life, sometimes for as long as they can.

The following sections look at two options available to those senior employees who do not want a clear-cut retirement: phased retirement and extending retirement.

Phased retirement

Phased retirement is an option that can mentally prepare someone for retirement. The exact format will depend on the organization and the individual but most schemes involve a reduction in hours or responsibility. The flexible working options usually associated with flexible retirement are part-time working and downshifting.

Reduction of hours is the most favoured option allowing the employee to have more time away from work to develop personal interests and hobbies. Downshifting involves a gradual reduction in responsibilities over time. This period can involve the training of a successor or may possibly involve changing jobs within the organization and/or moving to a lower grade, or a less pressurized environment.

The majority of employees approaching retirement prefer to continue with their usual role and it is often in the employer's interest to retain the skills and experience of their employee even if it is on a part-time basis.

Case study: Royal Bank of Scotland

Not all organizations will consider reducing a worker's hours on approach to retirement. George Hall found himself in this position and was seriously considering early retirement as an alternative to his high-stress role as a partner in a law firm.

Fortunately, Wealth Management, a division of the Royal Bank of Scotland Group had a requirement for a Senior Manager. The post was specifically advertised on a full- or part-time basis so as to attract someone with the required skills and experience.

George Hall applied for the position and secured the role on a part-time basis. Since joining RBS Group, George has settled into his new role and is enjoying having time outside of work to manage his personal affairs. He schedules his week by avoiding meetings on a Monday morning to give him time to prepare for the week ahead. George's clients are aware that he does not work on a Friday and are able to contact more junior staff should the need arise.

Extending retirement

For some the thought of stopping work in their early sixties is far from appealing. As a nation we are healthier, fitter and living longer and some older employees are keen to work beyond retirement. Equally some employers are keen to maintain their mature workforce. With the current skills shortage employers are realizing the benefits of retaining the expertise of those reaching retirement age and are devising attractive flexible options to allow them to continue to work either full- or part-time.

Barriers to flexible retirement

There are several reasons why those approaching retirement are reluctant to consider phased retirement.

- Financial considerations can be a major issue; the disincentive of lower pay along with pension considerations can make the option non-viable.
- There is also the psychological barrier; self-worth is often linked to status in the workplace and it is only natural for someone approaching retirement to want to maintain that status until they retire making phased retirement an unacceptable option.
- The stereotype of the older worker can still be a major issue; assumptions about outdated skill levels and accusations of blocking younger employees from advancing within an organization can be enough to push someone to retirement. This negative view of older workers can also impact on the introduction of policies designed to increase older workers' participation.

Even where flexible retirement options are encouraged, there are other fundamental reasons why a flexible retirement can be unsuitable.

Occupational pension funds

Up to 12 million UK employees are eligible for an additional company pension from their employers and 5 million current pensioners receive a retirement income from a company scheme.

There are two main types of company scheme:

- Final salary pension (also known as defined benefits pension) where at retirement, the pension received is based on final salary and linked to years of service with the company.
- Money purchase pension (also known as defined contributions pension) where the amount paid on retirement is dependent on the amount paid into the scheme by both the employer and employee.

If an employee has a final salary pension, working reduced hours on the run up to retirement is probably not an option. Equally someone on a money purchase pension may find that their pension falls short of that calculated if they are unable to make full contributions up to their retirement date. Their employer may also lower contributions if the employee is working fewer hours. Whatever pension scheme is in place it is advisable to take advice before altering the terms and conditions of employment (see Chapter 3 for further information on your rights at retirement).

At the time of writing, an occupational pension benefit cannot be paid to an employee while still working for the same employer (this may change with new legislation). This can make flexible retirement options unattractive if the employee is not able to supplement the reduced income with their pension benefits.

Sabbaticals

A sabbatical is a voluntary agreement between an employer and employee for the employee to take leave above their holiday allowance. Sabbaticals are usually taken by employees who want to travel, work for a charity, study, pursue a hobby or interest or simply have time to relax and recharge their batteries. From the perspective of the employee a sabbatical can provide a much-needed break. Even the most enthusiastic employee can become jaded but with some time away they can return rejuvenated.

Legally, an employee has no right to take a sabbatical and accordingly there is no specific legislation governing employee rights. Unlike other types of absence from work, such as sickness, holiday, maternity and parental leave, the employer is well within their rights to either grant or refuse a request for a sabbatical. Never the less, some employers do have policies in place defining terms and conditions for a sabbatical but this tends to be confined to larger organization.

Despite there being no legal requirement to oblige, more employers, large and small are starting to appreciate the benefits that a sabbatical can bring. A sabbatical can prove a cheap form of benefit with the majority of sabbaticals being unpaid and, from a more extreme perspective, they can also prove to be a useful way to reduce staff costs during a recession, rather than resorting to redundancy. Realistically, if an employer wants to retain a valuable member of the team they have little choice but to grant the request for the sabbatical. If they refuse the employee may well leave anyway.

TIP: If you are planning to take a sabbatical bear in mind, no one is indispensable. It is important to discuss with your employer what will happen on your return. The outcome of this conversation should be recorded and signed.

Case study: Maginus

Maginus is a small- to medium-sized enterprise (SME) specializing in software development. As an organization they are committed to flexible working offering a whole range of options to suit personal requirements. But undoubtedly their most flexible worker is a programmer who is currently living in Australia for six months. He is young and with career potential but wanted to travel. Maginus agreed a set piece of work that he could complete while on sabbatical in Australia. They also agreed to keep his job open for his return. This arrangement means that the company retains the skills of an experienced and valuable individual who will hopefully feel a greater bond of loyalty to the company on his return.

Maternity and paternity leave

At some point during a career an employee is likely to request time off to either have a baby or to help look after a child. The new Family Friendly Rights introduced in April 2003 have increased the amount of time that parents can legally take off work. The following provides brief guidance to the relevant statutory minimum rights:

- Maternity leave – up to one year of maternity leave can be taken, with 26 weeks of this period being paid.
- Paternity leave – a father is allowed to take two weeks' paid leave within eight weeks of a child's birth – the time must be taken in one week blocks – pay is currently £106 per week or 90% of average weekly earnings.
- Parental leave – parents who have at least one year's service are allowed up to 13 weeks' unpaid parental leave before the child is aged five.

For more information on these rights refer to the tailored interactive guidance on employee rights, or TIGER for short (www.tiger.gov.uk/). Non-employees should refer to Chapter 3, Your rights as a flexible worker, as you may not be entitled to these leave benefits.

The future of flexible working

The previous sections have provided an overview of the most common flexible working options available today. The list is far from exhaustive with new and inventive schemes being devised all the time. In the majority of cases employers are keen to maintain a contented and motivated workforce and requests for flexible working options that can be accommodated by the business are unlikely to be refused.

Less flexible organizations are likely to struggle in the coming years. Throughout Europe the demand for labour is rising and yet the number of people of traditional working age is shrinking. The consequence will be a smaller pool of labour and shortages in all areas. Organizations have already witnessed shortages of resource in certain skill areas and they are likely to see the same pattern with low skill employment areas.

The future is flexible, at least for some. Employers come in all shapes and sizes and it very much depends on the industry and sector as to whether a full range of flexible work options is on offer. Chapter 2 considers the types of organizations that have scope for flexibility. With the help of case studies this chapter will provide some guidance on how to plan your career if seeking flexibility in your working life.

Summary

The range of flexible working options available for workers is vast. There is flexibility around the hours worked, the type of working contract and the working location. There is also scope to take time out either for education, pleasure, family commitments or simply to recharge the batteries. This variety of flexible working options is partly due to the fact that demand for labour is high and supply is low; employees are in an ideal position to challenge the notion of a traditional working day. With shortages of labour in both skilled and non-skilled professions employers are keen to recruit and retain high calibre staff and are more open to proposals regarding flexible working solutions (as long as they fit the business needs).

This chapter has provided some food for thought, looking at the different flexible work options and considering appropriateness from both the employee and employer perspective. The following chapter will provide the next step, looking at whether flexible working is right for you.

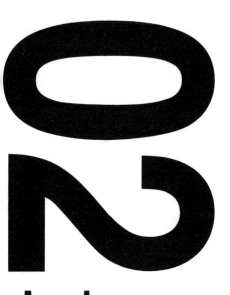

02

flexible working
– is it for you?

In this chapter you will learn:
- who is working flexibly
- what's in it for you and your employer
- whether you and your current role are suitable for flexible working
- how to convince your employer
- how to find a career that offers flexibility

Now that you are aware of at least some of the many flexible working options, the next step is deciding whether flexible working is the right choice for you.

This chapter will look at the attributes needed by both employee and employer in order to make flexible arrangements work well. For some roles and some industries flexibility just isn't an option. By considering your current role as well as roles within other industries you will have a clearer understanding of how you may need to develop your skills or possibly change your career path to secure your goal of a more flexible working life.

Who is working flexibly?

According to the National Statistics (www.statistics.gov.uk) there were 28 million employed workers in the UK at the end of 2002, the highest number on record. Of these, 7.1 million were part-time workers and 20.9 million full-time. Additionally there were 3.2 million self-employed workers giving a total workforce of 31.2 million.

There has been so much talk about flexible working in the media but what percentage of this 28 million employees have actually taken the plunge? Figures from 2003 indicate that 21 % of full-time employees have flexible working arrangements, but the percentages are different for men and women, with 18% of men and 27% of women doing so. For part-time workers the total proportion is 25%, with 17% for men and 27% for women.

What's in it for you?

So, for those who have taken up some form of flexible working, has the change to their work/life balance lived up to their expectations? John and Angie who both have flexible working lives certainly think so.

Case study: John and Angie

John works full-time for a community care home but his role allows him control over his working hours.

'My life would be impossible if I had to work standard hours. My wife is a part-time teacher and we have two girls of primary school age and we need the flexibility to be there for them at the beginning and end of the school day as well as holidays and times when they are off school with illnesses.

'I work full-time (37 hours), caring for adults with learning difficulties and criminal tendencies. We need to provide a continuous service 24 hours a day so the job entails shift work. I am also a trade union representative and 16 hours each week are dedicated to this role. Part of this time I work from home covering administration and making calls, the rest of the time I attend trade union meetings. It is up to me to organize my time. The remaining 21 hours that I spend at work are scheduled a month in advance. The hours vary depending on the cover needed but I quite often work two shifts over the weekend, which can fit in well with family commitments.'

John's wife Angie works for the local Education Authority helping refugee and asylum seeker children settle into local schools. Angie's role is a job share with both job share partners working 3 days a week.

'This is a new and exciting role and at the moment both my job share partner and I work the same 3 days a week. This is to give us the chance to get to know each other as well as providing the time to set up systems and working practices. Eventually I will work a set 3-day week, 2 days on my own with one double-up day so that we can keep each other up-to-date.

'Although my role is flexible there is also the stability of knowing what days I will be working. Previously I have worked as a supply teacher, which sometimes fitted around John's hours but not always. This arrangement is much better for all of us.'

Josie isn't so sure whether her flexible working arrangement has worked to her advantage. Having struggled to negotiate personal hours at the insurance company where she works, she now finds that organizing ad hoc childcare is more difficult than having a regular arrangement.

Case study: Josie

'At the time I felt victorious. I'd managed to negotiate a contract of 25 hours a week which I could fit around the needs of my family. This arrangement wasn't only for me, anyone could apply for what was called "personal hours".

'Two years on I'm not so convinced it works with my particular role. Some of the time it's fine, but not if I need to attend a morning meeting in London, or lunchtime meeting in York; within my working hours it's impossible. So having relaxed into the "luxury" of personalized working hours, I then need to find childcare to cover just the odd eventualities, which is more difficult than when it was a regular commitment; and children don't always realize the importance of it, either. As for trying to organize meetings between people who work similarly, that's incredibly awkward too and usually means that a meeting cannot take place for weeks and weeks. I know that teleconferencing has helped some larger companies, but not everyone can afford the technology (or can rely on their potential communicators to have the same level of technological investment either).'

Different circumstances can produce quite different reactions but Josie's experience shows that it can pay to think through both the pros and cons of a flexible working arrangement before you sign a new contract of employment.

In general, surveys and statistics suggest that flexible working arrangements provide a range of advantages; employees are said to benefit from:

- a happier disposition at both work and home
- greater responsibility and a sense of ownership
- better relations with management
- improved self-esteem, health, concentration and confidence
- improved loyalty and commitment
- having more time to focus on life outside work
- having greater control of their working lives.

What's in it for your employer?

Creating a more flexible working environment is far more than an employee perk. Evidence shows that when companies offer flexible arrangements they are rewarded by increased productivity, improved staff retention and lower absenteeism. It is also easier to recruit staff when a job is advertised with flexible hours.

In addition to improving staff morale and productivity there are also savings to be made if employees work from alternative locations. British Telecom (BT) claims to have saved around £52 million in overheads by introducing home working, proving that this form of flexible working can definitely benefit both employee and employer.

Are you suitable for flexible working?

The UK's labour market is increasingly concerned with having an improved work/life balance and working more flexibly is often considered to be the answer to all ailments. If the root of the problem is clearly not having enough hours in the day then flexible working may help. But, if the problem stems from your dissatisfaction with your job then flexible working may not solve your issues. It is important to make sure that you are moving to a more flexible working life for the right reasons.

The next step involves some self-analysis. You need to make sure that you have the right qualities, from an employer's perspective as well as from a personal viewpoint.

Is it for me?

The key qualities of a flexible worker are listed below. Do you have:

	Yes	No
• good self-discipline?	❏	❏
• strong communication skills?	❏	❏
• ability to work independently/in isolation?	❏	❏
• trustworthiness?	❏	❏
• mature attitude?	❏	❏
• commitment to the company?	❏	❏
• personal productivity in the office?	❏	❏

If you are still not sure whether you are suited to this type of
working refer to Chapter 5, The flexible working mindset, for a
more in-depth look at the qualities required to make a success
of working flexibly.

Could you work flexibly in your current role?

Not all roles are suitable for flexible working. You need to be
realistic in your expectations; there is little point putting in the
effort to apply for a flexible working arrangement if it is clearly
not an option.

Every job is different but there are three main attributes for a
role that lends itself to remote working, whether working from
home or working on the move:

1 The role should be made up of a number of independent tasks.
2 The role/task should have high information content, possibly
   involving administration or data handling tasks.
3 A manger should be able to supervise the role/task from a
   distance by setting objectives, time deadlines or financial
   budgets.

The majority of employees that work remotely do so on a part-
time basis so you should not discount this option if only some
of your tasks can be carried out away from your place of work.
For instance, you may be able to organize your working week
so that you spend some time at home completing the tasks that
do not need you to be office based.

Again, it is difficult to generalize but when it comes to working
reduced hours, the role needs to have some of the following
attributes:

1 The role should be made up of a number of independent tasks.
2 The tasks that make up the role should be able to be carried
   out by more than one person.
3 The role should not suffer due to lack of continuity.

If you want to reduce your hours you may need to convince your employer that there is a subset of tasks that can be adequately managed in an alternative way, either by refining the role or passing on some tasks to another employee.

A role or task does not necessarily need all the attributes listed to be a candidate for flexible working and equally, each type of flexible working arrangement will have its own demands. The best way to assess your job is to keep a log of how you are spending your time and then evaluate each task in turn. This log can then be used to demonstrate to your employer the impact that your request for flexible working will have on the organization and your colleagues.

Exercise

Take an average working week and keep a record of all your tasks. If you are considering working remotely, identify all those tasks that you could carry out from home or from a remote location. If you intend to reduce your hours, make a note of those tasks that could be carried out by another member of staff. If there is no such thing as an average week in your current role you may need to complete this exercise over a period of a month.

The following is an example record for Claire, a clerical officer who wants to work from home for part of the working week. She has indicated all those tasks that she could complete at home and those that could only be carried out at the office.

Day	Time	Task	Home	Office
Monday	9–10	Filing		✓
	10–11.30	Correspondence	✓	
	11.30–12.30	Filing		✓
	1.30–4	Statistical analysis	✓	
	4–5	Correspondence	✓	
Tuesday	9–10	Weekly staff meeting		✓
	10–12.30	Minutes/Action list	✓	
	1.30–5	Statistical analysis	✓	
Wednesday	9–10	Progress meeting with Manager		✓

	10–12.30	Correspondence	✓	
	1.30–2	Shorthand		✓
	2–3	Correspondence	✓	
	3–5	Statistical analysis	✓	
Thursday	9–5	Statistical analysis	✓	
Friday	9–11	Produce weekly report (with Linda)		✓
	11–12.30	filing		✓
	1.30–3	Statistical analysis	✓	
	3–5	Correspondence	✓	

By reorganizing some tasks, it is feasible that Claire could work from home for at least two days a week. This data will help her make a case when she approaches her employer with the request.

Convincing your employer

On the face of it some jobs don't lend themselves to flexible working – if you work as a cleaner or a traffic warden you can hardly work from home. Nevertheless, in some cases there is scope for an imaginative approach – a cleaner may be able to work flexible hours or a traffic warden complete their paperwork at home. Regardless of your role, if you have a small child or a disabled dependant under 18 your employer has to take your request seriously and respond even if the answer is no.

Self check

Before you launch in take the time to prepare your case.

- Think carefully about what you really want and whether it will work for you. ❏
- Gather information – find out if your organization has a flexible working policy – what flexible arrangements does it support? ❏
- Seek advice – if you belong to a trade union, contact your local representative before you

approach your employer – ask whether they have
experience of advising on similar requests to yours. ❏

- Gather experience – you may know someone who
  has made the switch to working flexibly – this could
  be someone in your workplace or someone working
  for a different organization – talk to them to see if
  they can give you the benefit of their experience. ❏
- Make a list of some of the ways in which your
  organization can benefit from flexible working. ❏
- Produce a plan – set out clearly and concisely the
  benefits to you and to the organization. ❏
- Consider building a review period into your plan
  so that both you and your employer can discuss
  whether flexible working is meeting your needs
  (and the needs of your organization) or whether it
  could be refined. ❏

TIP: Hopefully you will receive a positive response but if you
feel that the outcome is not reasonable there are steps you can
take. See Chapter 3, Your rights as a flexible worker.

Searching for a career that offers flexibility

If your current role is unable to provide the flexibility you
desire, you may need to seriously consider finding a new
employer or even contemplate a change of career. Looking for a
new job is never easy but when you have the added constraint
of wanting a job that offers flexibility the search can become
even harder.

Business location

If you want to work flexibly where is the best geographical
location to start your job hunt? With 85% of the entire UK
business population (3.8 million) based within England, and
London and the South East accounting for nearly 1.3 million of
these businesses (35% of the UK total), statistically there has to
be more chance of securing a job (with or without flexible
working options) in these areas. But if you live elsewhere in the

UK, don't despair. Statistics show that, based on the percentage of the working population, the number of both men and women working flexibly are fairly consistent throughout the country. In fact the North East of England boasts the highest percentage of women working flexibly (29.9%) with Wales and Scotland having over 21% of their male employee population working on a flexible basis.

Business size

Businesses come in three sizes, small, medium and large. The Department of Trade and Industry (DTI) loosely defines a small organization as having 0 to 49 employees, a medium-sized enterprise as having 50 to 249 employees and a large company as having over 250 employees. The DTI estimated that of the 3.8 million businesses in the UK at the start of 2002 almost all of these (99.1%) were classified as small with only 27,000 of medium size and 7,000 large companies. These figures show that the vast majority of businesses can be classified as small- to medium-sized enterprises (SMEs). Statistics also show that the majority (55.6%) of all employees work for an SME.

So if you want to work flexibly are you better to aim for a large corporate or a small, family-run business? Unfortunately, there is no clear answer to this. Although larger companies have the infrastructure to organize flexible working options, some small organizations provide outstanding examples of true flexibility; particularly those owned or managed by people who themselves demand a decent work/life balance. Equally some large corporate organizations are lagging way behind the times, hesitant to provide flexibility for fear of losing control. In many cases, size is irrelevant to the flexible arrangements that are available to staff; it is more often the culture of the organization that determines the level of flexibility.

What sectors/industries are offering flexible working?

There is scope for flexible working in most organizations but some industries are certainly more flexible than others. A study by the DTI found the construction industry to be the least flexible sector of the economy with just 5% of sites offering reduced hours. Agriculture, fishing and mining featured second lowest with just 11% offering flexibility to employees. As for the best type of organization to target, research conducted by

Shirley Dex and Colin Smith at the Judge Institute of Management, Cambridge University, found that non-managers are more likely to be offered flexible working if they work for a large, public sector organization that has affiliations with recognized unions. Failing this they suggest that you look for an organization that offers good human resources policies. According to the research, an organization that has a strong HR department is more likely to offer flexible working arrangements.

Alternatively, try to find an organization that has developed a culture that embraces flexibility and is actively taking steps to encourage the workforce to consider their work/life balance. Back in 2002, the DTI announced government funding to help more than three-quarters of a million employees reach a better work/life balance. The initiative involved 91 private, 109 public and 33 voluntary organizations with each receiving a share of the £4.8 million funding. The scheme is designed to provide free work/life balance consultancy and support to help organizations develop flexible working initiatives. British Airways, Tesco, Age Concern and The Prince's Trust are just a few of the larger organizations who qualified for the fund; for a list of all 233 organizations, access http://164.36.164.20/work-lifebalance/press_8802a.html. This could prove a good starting point for your job hunting.

If you are contemplating a career change, take the time to read the following sections. They provide an overview of just some of the many sectors and industries that contribute to the UK economy.

The public sector

The UK's largest employer is the public sector. Public sector organizations employ around 5 million people and although they are renowned for having a rigid, slow-changing culture that does not always lend itself to flexible working, things are changing.

There has been a strong Civil Service policy commitment to improving work/life balance over the last few years, which has resulted in an increase in the number of staff working flexibly. The Civil Service, made up of over 170 departments and agencies, countrywide, employs almost half a million people (about 2% of the employed population and 10% of all public sector employees). It is often the perception that all Civil Servants work in London but in fact only one in five do. For current career opportunities take a look at www.careers.civil-service.gov.uk.

County and district councils are often ahead of the field when it comes to flexibility in the workplace. In most of the UK there are two tiers of local government: county councils and district councils. Larger towns and cities have just one council providing all the functions of the two. The majority of councils have their own websites detailing employment opportunities.

Case study: Surrey Country Council

'To Surrey County Council (SCC), flexible working means working in the most appropriate place, at the most appropriate time, in the most appropriate way to support improved delivery of services to the public.' (Carol Mack, SCC)

The Surrey County Council Workstyle project was a response to the pressure to find significant cash savings while protecting front line services from cuts. As well as achieving savings by rationalizing the property portfolio, the project also involved a change in culture. Instead of having fixed places of work, one desk per person and separate IT networks, they moved to a much more flexible way of working.

The project has resulted in SCC acquiring a number of high quality office premises across the county including a new HQ. The local offices are designed to ease the problems of driving to a central location, cutting down on travel time and the associated stress. The buildings are all fully serviced and provide meeting rooms, quiet rooms, relaxation areas as well as reprographics facilities. Staff are able to work from any SCC building and apart from a small number of desks for core office based staff, individuals are encouraged to desk share with other staff working and living in the same area.

With the new investments in technology, staff can access software and data from any PC within the region. As well as allowing staff to work remotely at satellite offices, these advances in technology have also enabled staff to be home-based or mobile, working alongside customers using tablets (small hand-held devices).

These new ways of working have meant changes. Staff are quickly appreciating that communication is key and managers are learning to measure staff outputs as a means of assessing performance rather than considering hours worked.

From a business perspective, the project is meeting the objectives. SCC's reputation for offering flexible working has helped recruitment and staff retention; flexible working is often high on the list of considerations for potential and existing employees, alongside work satisfaction, team working, benefits and pay.

As for the staff, being freed from the 9 to 5 working pattern has been welcomed by many; staff now have more of a choice over their working hours. Instead of offering a single flexible option, Surrey County Council has found that a mixed menu approach delivers the best fit between organizational and personal needs. For instance, combining hot desking, with home working and some flexibility with work hours enables staff to manage work demands, respond better to service needs and, at the same time, meet their personal needs.

Retailing

Retailing is the UK's largest employer outside the public sector with 11% of all employees (2.7 million people) involved in the industry. Retailing is the place to be if you can manage shift work and flexible hours. Our consumer society is no longer prepared to accept a retail industry that operates 9 to 5, 5 days a week (with half-day closing on a Wednesday). Some of us want to shop 24 hours a day, 7 days a week, 364 days a year; and with our multicultural society some shops even open on Christmas Day.

The majority of retail outlets provide a whole menu of innovative flexible schemes from grandparent leave (where grandparents have paid leave to help out with new grandchildren) to 'Benidorm' leave, an option for the over 50s who fancy a couple of months in the sun. The larger retail chains all seem to have a similar approach to the flexible working arrangements offered by Sainsburys.

Case study: Sainsburys

Established in 1869, Sainsburys now operates 24 hours a day, 364 days a year making flexible working essential to business success. In the UK, Sainsburys employs 142,000 staff with around 70% of employees working part-time. Sainsburys' flexible working policy applies across all parts of the business and includes a full range of options. Part-time hours range from 8 to

36 hours per week with staff choosing a variety of hours per day and days per week. They also offer term-time and dual store contracts where parents can choose to work during school terms only, and university students can transfer to a different store close to their family homes in holiday periods. Career break schemes of up to 1 year are also available for personal development or caring responsibilities.

Sainsburys believes that it is important for staff to take the lead when shaping their work/life balance. Anyone is able to suggest to their line manager a working pattern that would suit them, and as long as there is a strong business case and it fits in with colleagues, it will be seriously considered.

Hospitality, leisure and media

The hospitality, leisure and media industries are certainly not renowned for their 9 to 5 cultures. By the very nature of these industries, employees need to work when the rest of the population are enjoying their leisure time.

Hospitality

The hospitality sector is ideal for those seeking a flexible working life. It is one of the main engines for growth in the UK with forecasts for sustained growth over the next few years. The industry employs over 1.8 million people in the UK, working in around 300,000 establishments. Demand for quality staff is high, with skill shortages being the major issue facing the sector today. Skilled chefs and managers are in great demand and staff turnover remains high.

Leisure

If you choose to work in the leisure industry you are going to be working so others can relax. This means 'unsociable' working hours, often involving weekends and public holidays. Unfortunately, pay and conditions do not usually reflect the demand for out-of-hours working but for those who choose this industry the social interaction and perks of using facilities or equipment can compensate.

The media

The media industry is competitive and demanding, often involving long hours and time away from home. Flexible working features in all areas, with up to a quarter of the workforce being employed on a freelance basis at any one time. If you are keen to work as a freelancer, the best options are TV production, film and video. Freelance work is less common in interactive media, radio and engineering roles.

Financial sector

Working in the financial sector has not entirely lost its 'traditional' air. Many of the roles are client facing. However, work/life balance has become an issue in recent years and some of the larger employers are taking steps to address this.

Case study: Royal Bank of Scotland

Founded in Edinburgh, Scotland in 1727 the Royal Bank of Scotland Group has grown to be one of the world's leading financial services providers ranked, by market capitalization, as the second largest bank in the UK and Europe and as the fifth largest in the world.

RBS has grown through acquisitions, notably with the takeover of National Westminster Bank in 2000. Growth always brings challenges but growth by acquisition can have the added issues of merging cultures. RBS has coped well with change and has been keen to embrace flexible working. When faced with the government's 2003 legislation, RBS decided to extend their commitment by offering the right to request flexible working to all staff rather than just to those carers specified by the legislation. To increase awareness of the flexible options available, they also introduced a suite of flexible working policies in 2003 that they named Yourtime. Yourtime provides a number of core policies such as job sharing, phasing back to work after maternity or adoption leave, part-time work and variable hours. In addition there are several non-core flexible options that can be adopted at the discretion of the individual businesses – these are compressed hours, home working and term-time working.

Another bank, HBOS, formerly the Halifax Building Society and the Bank of Scotland, has recently introduced an innovative flexible working package for their Retail Contact Centres. The scheme has been named 'Flextra' and it is designed to improve the working conditions of the staff that deal with customer enquiries via the telephone. It is available for full-time employees as well as part-time employees who work a choice of fixed shifts covering peak times.

The scheme offers a range of benefits that include: trading off certain aspects of their working pattern for another; a variety of changes to shift working; time banking, so as to build up time off in lieu; term-time working; choice of lunch breaks; and taking specified days off.

Manufacturing

The British manufacturing industry is currently going through its worst recession since the early 1990s. There are 3.8 million people employed in manufacturing in the UK, around 14% of the working population; but the industry is believed to be shedding jobs at the rate of about 10,000 a month. If you compare this to the service industries where there are over 20 million employed; it may appear that manufacturing is a dying industry but jobs in service industries depend on manufacturing and the government is convinced that modern manufacturing is central to our future. They are confident that with new technologies manufacturing can survive and prosper in the long term.

This is a sector that provides a wide range of opportunities and working conditions. From companies employing just a few staff to huge multinationals employing as many as 100,000 people worldwide, cultures vary greatly. The flexible working options available will depend on the culture of the organization as well as the practical considerations of the manufacturing process. Manufacturing is renowned for using shift working to ensure maximum productivity as well as introducing annualized hours schemes to manage peaks and troughs in production. This may well give the impression that flexibility in the manufacturing industry is a one-way process but this following extract from the website of a manufacturing industry gives hope for the future.

Case study: Listawood

'The people who had nothing to lose in working for Listawood were the mothers of small children trapped in our village by poor transport and lack of affordable childcare. In fact they were very keen to get a few hours in adult company and earn some money, but most of all they wanted to be able to work around the needs of their family. Although they wouldn't have used the terminology, they were very clear on the issue of Work–Life balance. We were so glad to get the help that we weren't bothered if they started work after they had dropped children off at school or finished early...

'Above all, it wasn't a problem if a child was ill and mother had to stay at home. No mother ever had to ring us up pretending to be ill, when actually it was her child who was sick. They could tell the truth. It wasn't a problem. If you have got the main responsibility of looking after young children, you know how important this is.

'We gradually realised that for many staff our family friendly policies were of vital importance; they wanted ways in which they could look after their own children. It never occurred to us that working part-time should be a barrier to training or responsibility. In fact the company was built through the work of part-time mothers rejoining the workforce as their children grew up. Many of our team leaders, including the Production Director, joined the company as part-timers and have contributed enormously to the company's development.'

You may be forgiven for thinking that Listawood is a small, local company without ambitions, but this is far from the case. Although it started with just £500 in the bank in 1987, Listawood has diversified into a cluster of a dozen related businesses with common values and shared resources. Just as a flavour of their success, the award winning Listawood is Europe's largest producer of computer mouse mats and the UK market leader in promotional computer mice (www.listawood.com).

Voluntary sector

Voluntary organizations deal with every conceivable area of civil society and can be classified as either charities or non-profit making organizations. Around 569,000 people were working in the voluntary sector in 2002, which equates to about 2% of the total employed UK workforce.

Female workers traditionally dominate this sector with almost two-thirds of employees being women. The voluntary workforce comprises paid staff and volunteers with a large majority of voluntary organizations relying solely on volunteers. Paid staff are typically subject to short-term contracts and poor levels of job security due to the short-term nature of funding contracts. However, if job security is not a concern you will find that there is compensation to be found in the high degree of personal flexibility afforded by some organizations.

Case study: National charity

Nadia works as a District Organizer for a national charity. Fortunately for Nadia the post is permanent as it is funded centrally and she has been able to negotiate a degree of flexibility that would be the envy of many.

'I work a job share, with flexible working hours and I am based at home. My job share partner was working full-time (37 hours a week) but when she returned from maternity leave she asked to work part-time. I applied for the job share and now we split the hours 50:50. We cover a specific region so we also split the area geographically. The only time we work together is to run conferences and training sessions.

I can work my hours when I like so I schedule meetings to suit my personal commitments where possible. I do all my admin and phoning from home and usually only pop into the local office once a week.'

Health and social care

The latest figures (November 2003) show that The National Health Service (NHS) employed approximately 1.2 million people in September 2002. Private healthcare organizations are estimated to employ a further 750,000 people, and over 100,000 other individuals are delivering complementary medicine and therapies. A further 1.2 million staff work in social care dealing with other personal needs, such as emotional well-being, poverty, life changes, life crises and life decisions.

Life as a health worker can be demanding, stressful but also rewarding. As with the majority of the caring professions the workforce has a strong female presence, which has resulted in the need to introduce flexible working options to recruit and retain staff. For further information on all the areas of social care visit the General Social Care Council's website at www.gscc.org.uk. For information on careers in the NHS access www.nhs.uk.

Case study: The NHS

NHS employers are committed to improving the working lives of all staff within the NHS, where women make up over 70% of the workforce. They have introduced Improving Working Lives (IWL), a standard by which NHS employers and their staff can measure their organization's HR management. NHS organizations should have achieved accreditation against the Standard by April 2003, by demonstrating improvement to the working lives of their staff. As part of a continuous improvement initiative, all organizations are required to meet Practice Plus status by 31 March 2006.

Although, on the whole the scheme appears to have been successful, evidence suggests that the IWL initiative seems to have passed doctors by with many doctors being unaware that the scheme also applies to them. Long hours culture is still entrenched in the NHS, particularly for doctors. To attempt to rectify this, the Department of Health has set up, and substantially funded, a Flexible Career Scheme designed to enable doctors who wish to work flexibly to do so. However, when asked, doctors still feel that demand for part-time/flexible jobs outstrips supply.

The IWL provides NHS staff with the full range of flexible working opportunities available in most industries, such as part-time work, job share and compressed hours. In addition, the NHS operates a Staff Bank for Administration and Clerical roles as well as Nursing and Midwifery staff. Staff are employed on a flexible 'as needed' basis. They receive weekly pay, paid annual leave, occupational health support and have the opportunity to contribute to the NHS Pension Scheme. They also receive on-going training and support, both mandatory and optional.

Flexible retirement is a national scheme that provides NHS staff with early and part-time retirement options. There are currently around 150,000 NHS staff who are aged 50 or more, 50,000 of these are nurses. Each year between 4,000 and 5,000 nurses retire from the NHS. Two-thirds leave aged 60 or less with most being in good health and able to continue working if they wished.

The NHS aims to encourage these experienced people to consider retirement options to help the NHS meet demand particularly at critical times of the year such as the winter months. There are currently three schemes in place, wind down, step down and retire and come back.

- Wind down is an alternative to retiring by reducing the hours worked in the current post in ways that do not reduce pension benefits.

- Step down is an option to move to a less demanding, lower paid role in a way that preserves pension entitlement from the higher-level post.
- Retire and come back is an option where you retire and start receiving your pension but return to carry on with part-time or full-time work in the long or short term.

Education

Teaching or working within an educational establishment has always been an option for those who want flexibility. The education sector can be divided into three main areas, School education, Further Education (FE) and Higher Education (HE). All three areas offer a high degree of flexibility for both academic and support staff and are ideal occupations for those with children, who need to take time off to coincide with school holidays.

Job share is a fairly common option within schools with teachers typically working a two and a half day week. In some cases the job share teacher will be available to cover for absent colleagues during their non-working days, which can certainly benefit the school. It is also quite common for Teaching Assistants and support staff to negotiate part-time hours with the ultimate flexibility being had by supply teachers who usually work for an agency and only work on a temporary basis to cover for teachers who are ill or on maternity leave.

FE colleges operate in a similar way to schools and provide the same opportunities for flexibility. In addition there is also scope for part-time lecturers to work during the evenings and weekends to teach courses designed for those who are working during normal college hours.

Higher Education employs over 300,000 people, equating to around 1.8% of the total UK workforce. Universities and colleges play an important role in the economic, social and cultural development of their regions. They are often major employers in towns and cities with larger institutions employing over 5,000 staff. Academic staff make up about 45% of this number with non-academic staff accounting for the remaining 55%, working in positions in libraries, human resources, finance, estates management, residential and commercial services, scientific and technical support, leisure, counselling, security, purchasing, marketing and public relations.

Information technology and communications

IT often has a 'long hours' reputation, the cyclical nature of projects means that extra work may be necessary to meet project deadlines or to provide support. Flexible working is helping the situation with a survey of the IT industry carried out by the DTI in March 2004 reporting that roughly half of the respondents already work a flexible work schedule.

Case study: BT

BT is an obvious example of an IT and communications organization that has successfully introduced flexibility into the workplace. Employing over 116,000 people in the UK and Europe, the BT Group actively encourages flexible working with a strong emphasis on home working schemes. The company supplies everything staff need to create the office at home including computer, fax, furniture and the technology to communicate with the office and customers.

BT is keen to recruit and retain employees who have childcare commitments. They have negotiated a number of contracts with external suppliers of childcare at a reduced cost and BT Group Women's Network job share register has been set up to match sharers. For careers information, access www.bt.com/careers.

It's not just the large IT companies that have adopted flexible work patterns, as some smaller organizations have found that they also need to adapt to grow and develop.

Case study: Maginus

At the time when they first considered introducing formal flexible working policies Maginus was a relatively small firm employing just 90 staff. This progressive software house already had ad hoc arrangements in place between individuals and their managers, and, on the surface it seemed to be working fine. But underneath the apparent flexibility there was a growing unease among staff. Some were resentful that the arrangement was not available to everyone, while those who were working flexibly felt that it wasn't recognized as a legitimate option, and that they owed the company for their preferential treatment.

Change was needed and a formal policy was introduced offering differing degrees of flexibility within the three types of job role: sales, project implementation and customer support.

As a result of these initiatives 35% of staff now work from home, and 25% have changed their hours. The new policy has been universally accepted by staff and has provided greater openness and equality within the company. Flexibility is available to all, with the format depending on the individual's role, the team they work in and their own skills and ability. The policy stipulates conditions such as core hours and the requirement to take an hour's lunch break for health and safety reasons. It also clarifies some grey areas, including a proviso that home workers cannot provide childcare at the same time as working, the working hours must be focused totally on work. (However, they can fit in some responsibilities such as collecting children from school. Some employees, for example, stop work at 3pm to pick up children, but work again from 8 to 10pm when the children are in bed.)

In the first year of these new policies productivity, measured in customer project days generating revenue, has increased by 8%. Overtime costs have nearly halved, from 2.19% of total salary bill to 1.2%. Absenteeism has dropped to 2.4%, staff turnover from 11 to 2% and all four women on maternity leave over the period have returned to work.

Summary

Hopefully, by now you have decided whether you are right for flexible working and equally whether flexible working is right for you. If you already have a role that lends itself to flexibility then all you need to do is state your case. If you have to look further afield then you will need to find an organization that can provide the level of flexibility that you require.

It is difficult to provide a profile of the type of organization that embraces flexible working. It seems to very much depend on the culture of the company rather than size or geographical location. Organizations where the benefits of a work/life balance are appreciated from the top down are more likely to encourage flexible working arrangements. If an organization has a boss who takes the time to attend his child's sports day or comes in late a couple of mornings a week because she has been to the gym you are more likely to find that flexible working is a reality and not just a document that gathers dust.

As the previous sections have shown, some sectors of the economy are more flexible that others purely due to the practicalities of the business. If you are thinking of changing jobs or moving to a new career, spend some time researching the market before you take that leap.

03

your rights as a flexible worker

In this chapter you will learn:
- about existing legislation affecting flexible working
- about future legislation
- about the rights of workers and those in retirement

In their 2000 Work/Life Balance campaign the UK government outlined the benefits of allowing employees the opportunity to veer away from a traditional '9 to 5' working pattern towards working on a more flexible basis. More recently this move towards creating a more flexible workforce has seen the adoption of the European Flexible Working Directive in 2003 which is due to be reviewed and broadened in 2006. The self-employed and agency workers have also been embraced within this changing culture with the Fixed-Term Employees (Prevention of Less Favourable Treatment) Regulations that came into force on 1 October 2002 and talks are in progress to secure equality for temporary workers.

While the benefits to the individual are fairly obvious, many employers have remained resistant to change, not appreciating that work/life balance initiatives can save them large sums of money in recruitment, retention and development expenses as well as producing huge savings in accommodation costs.

But with government figures showing that around 3 million workers (one-eighth of the workforce) are also primary carers, the demand for flexibility in the workplace cannot be ignored. Employers have little choice but to wake up to the fact that legislation is pushing them towards a more flexible way of working.

This chapter will first look at the Minimum Wage and Working Time Regulations. These regulations impact on all workers, whether full- or part-time employees or contract workers. Subsequent sections look specifically at the rights of different groups of workers from the employed to those working on fixed-term or temporary contracts.

The National Minimum Wage

The National Minimum Wage is designed to set the minimum acceptable hourly rate of pay. The rates are based on the recommendations of the independent Low Pay Commission. The main (adult) rate is for workers aged 22 and over, and the development rate is for workers aged 18–21 inclusive. The development rate can also apply to workers aged 22 and above during their first 6 months in a new job with a new employer if they are receiving accredited training.

Working Time Regulations

October 1998 saw the introduction of regulations relating to the hours that can legally be worked throughout the European Union. These new regulations represented a dramatic change for the UK, where historically working time has been subject to little legal regulation.

The Working Time Regulations (WTR) apply to those provided with a contract of employment (the employed) as well as those working under more temporary contracts such as agency workers, temps and freelancers. The WTR do not apply to the self-employed and there are also other exemptions including those working within transport, those working at sea and doctors in training. There are also some special provisions for adolescent workers who are over the minimum school leaving age but less than 18 years of age

In brief, the WTR state the following:

- The working week should be limited to an average of 48 hours.
- Night workers should be limited to working an average of 8 hours in each 24-hour period.
- Night workers whose work involves special hazards or heavy physical or mental strain should work no more than 8 hours for each 24-hour period.
- Adult night workers are entitled to a health assessment before being required to perform night work and periodically thereafter.
- Adolescent workers are entitled to a health and capacities assessment before being required to perform night work and periodically thereafter.
- Adult workers are entitled to one day off each week.
- Adolescent workers are entitled to two days off.
- Adult workers are entitled to 11 hours' consecutive rest per day.
- Adolescent workers are entitled to 12 hours' consecutive rest per day.

For full details of the WTR access the Department of Trade and Industry (DTI) website at www.dti.gov.uk/er/work_time_regs.

The sectors that are excluded from the regulations were made exempt because the European Commission (EC) and EU member states agreed that these sectors would require their own special rules. The UK government has since introduced measures to extend WTR to these sectors. Details of sectors that are exempt and the special measures that are in place for these sectors can be found at www.dti.gov.uk/er/work_time_regs/exsectors.htm.

The opt-out clause

If you are working for a UK organization there is an opt-out clause in the WRT. The opt-out provides an opportunity for employees to work more than an average working week of 48 hours if they have agreed to do so with employers.

However the 'opt-out' is not popular with the rest of the EU or the UK trade unions. The unions claim that the opt-out is being abused with more than 3 million men in the UK working in excess of 48 hours a week. This equates to almost one in four of the male workforce. The figure for women is much lower mainly due to the fact that more women work part-time. Statistics show that around 5.5% of the female workforce works more than 48 hours each week.

At the time of writing the opt-out is still in place but its fate is in the hands of the European Commission (EC) who is likely to announce a decision in the near future.

The EC has outlined four options for the future of the opt-out:

1 Phasing out of the opt-out.
2 Clamping down on the alleged abuse by employers.
3 Only allowing the opt-out where there is an agreement between employers and unions or the workforce as a whole.
4 Individual employees can continue to put in more than an average working week of 48 hours if they have agreed to do so with their employer (as is).

Although the statistics show that a quarter of the UK male workforce work excessive hours, in fact the average number of full-time hours worked has fallen to an all-time low of 37.1 hours per week, down from 38.9 hours 10 years ago. For part-time workers, the average is 15.5 hours a week. This downward trend has been gradual but statistics show that it has accelerated over the past few years as a result of the working time regulations. Statisticians believe the trend is likely to continue.

Your rights as an employee

At the moment only certain employees have the right to request a flexible working arrangement but some forward-thinking organizations are already extending the offering to all or part of their workforce. The media is continually reporting on new initiatives being discussed by the government and it is likely that current legislation will be extended to include more of the working population.

The European Flexible Working Directive

The European Flexible Working Directive, which came into effect in the UK on 6 April 2003, allows employees with children under the age of 6 or disabled children aged under 18 to apply for flexible working arrangements. This law merely gives employees the right to apply for flexible arrangements, it does not provide the automatic right for such requests to be granted. By law, employers must comply with the statutory timetable in responding to employees but they are within their rights to refuse a request to work flexibly for business-related reasons.

Who can apply for flexible working?

The new regulations come with a set of rules and anyone wanting to apply for flexible working must satisfy the following conditions. If you are considering requesting a flexible working arrangement, first check that you are eligible.

Self check

The applicant must:

- be an employee who has a contract of employment (agency workers and members of the armed forces are not eligible)   ❏
- have a child under the age of 6 or a disabled child under 18   ❏
- have parental responsibility for the child (this includes biological parents, legal guardians, adoptive and foster parents – including same sex partners)   ❏
- be making the application in order to be able to care for the child   ❏

- have worked for their employer for a period of 26 continuous weeks at the time the application is made ☐
- have not made a previous application to work flexibly during the past 12 months. ☐

How to apply

Once you have decided that you are eligible the next step is to formally apply to your employer. To do this you must put your case in writing:

- State that the application is being made under the statutory right to apply for flexible working.
- Provide details of your relationship to the child.
- Provide an outline of your proposal giving details of how it will affect your employer's business and how this may be dealt with.
- Specify a start date for the proposed change allowing a reasonable amount time for your employer to consider the proposal and implement it.
- State whether a previous application has been made and if so the date on which it was made.
- Remember to date your application.

Refer to Chapter 2, Flexible working – is it for you?, for more information on preparing your case.

TIP: Once your employer has approved your application your terms and conditions of employment will be changed and you may have no automatic right to change back to your previous pattern of work. If this is a concern you may be able to incorporate a change back clause in your contract if your employer is in agreement.

The employer response

Once you have applied for flexible working it is your employer's duty to:

- notify you in writing that they have agreed to your request within 28 days of receiving your application

or

- arrange to meet with you within 28 days of receiving your application to discuss you application

- allow you to be accompanied by a work colleague at that meeting
- notify you of their decision within 14 days of the date of the meeting.

There are three likely outcomes. Your employer will either:

- accept your request and inform you of the start date
- confirm a compromise that was agreed at the meeting

or

- reject the request setting out clear business reasons for doing so as well as the steps you can take to appeal against their decision.

What to do if your request is refused

Requests can be turned down for a number of reasons, including potential harm to the business, or the burden of additional costs. But the law prohibits companies from ignoring requests or having a blanket ban on flexible working. In general applications for flexible working arrangements can only be refused for the following reasons:

- the burden of additional costs
- detrimental effect on ability to meet customer demand
- inability to reorganize work among existing staff
- inability to recruit additional staff
- detrimental impact on quality
- detrimental impact on performance.

If you are refused and decide to appeal the appeal should be heard within 14 days of your application. A work colleague can accompany you to the appeal and you should be notified of the decision within 14 days. The notification will either:

- uphold the appeal
- specify any agreed variations and the start date

or

- dismiss the appeal explaining the grounds for the decision.

If your appeal is dismissed and you are not satisfied with the outcome there are a number of options open to you. The first route is to try to find a solution internally by discussing the issues with your employer informally or using the internal grievance procedures. If you feel you need help, you are quite within your rights to ask a trade union representative or other qualified person to attend meetings with you.

If all else fails you can refer your grievance to an employment tribunal, or as an alternative use the services of the Acas Arbitration Scheme. As long as both parties agree, the Acas Arbitration Scheme can be used to resolve the dispute in England, Wales and now Scotland (since April 2004). This scheme is designed to be speedy and informal with an arbitrator hearing the case and making a decision that is binding for both parties.

TIP: If you opt for the Acas Arbitration Scheme and don't like the outcome you do not have the right to then go to an employment tribunal. The remedies and compensation that an arbitrator can award are the same as those of an employment tribunal.

If you decide to take your case to an employment tribunal you must do so within 3 months of your appeal being refused. Complaints can be made to an employment tribunal on the following grounds:

• the employer's failure to comply with the statutory procedure
• the employer's use of an incorrect fact to explain why the application has been refused and which the employer failed to address at the appeal
• the employer's refusal to allow the employee to be accompanied.

If a decision is made against your employer by either an employment tribunal or an Acas arbitrator, your employer may be ordered to accept your application for flexible working. In some cases you may also be entitled to compensation. The tribunal or the Acas arbitrator will determine the amount of compensation due, up to a maximum payment of 8 weeks' pay.

For further information on the Acas Arbitration Scheme access their website at www.acas.org.uk/rights/emprights_info.html#2 or telephone the Acas Hotline on 08457 474747.

Future legislation for flexible working

A survey carried out by the DTI one year after the introduction of the European Flexible Working Directive showed that up to 24% of those eligible had applied for a more flexible working life. The same survey showed that almost 80% of those who had applied had been granted the option whereas the charity Working Families claims that the figure is nearer 60% (www.workingfamilies.org.uk).

The apparent success of the scheme produced a further announcement in April 2004, when the Prime Minister confirmed that the Labour government has future plans to extend the regulations to offer the right to apply for flexible working to up to 5 million carers looking after elderly parents, infirm relatives or close friends. The Prime Minister is keen to find ways to support carers appreciating that an ageing population will create a growing pressure on employees who are looking after an elderly parent or relative. The impact of the current legislation is being continuously reviewed, but the government currently states that there will be no further changes to the legislation until after a formal review in 2006. Details of the government's monitoring can be found at www.dti.gov.uk/er/individual/workparents_mon.htm.

One of the other new initiatives being considered by the government is a service to help working parents negotiate flexible working conditions. By providing a personal adviser it is hoped that more parents will be able to find a solution to enable them to combine work and childcare. The Conservative Party is also keen to promote flexibility in the workplace with a recent report stating that, if elected, it will consider paying grandparents to look after children, thus enabling parents to work. It seems that regardless of the outcome of the 2005 general election flexible working will certainly feature on the agenda.

Contract of employment for flexible workers

As an employee you should have a written contract detailing the terms and conditions of employment. If recruited into a role requiring flexible working your terms and conditions should state exactly how the arrangement works. If you are changing to a flexible working pattern, either at your own request or the request of your employer, your terms and conditions of employment need to be updated to reflect the changes.

You may find that within your organization flexible working arrangements are organized on a much more informal basis. An arrangement to leave early on a Friday but come in early on a Monday, or the long lunch break on a Wednesday to enable you to pursue an out of work hobby; these arrangements may be authorized by your current line manager but in many cases these ad hoc arrangements have not been sanctioned by senior managers and are only based on a verbal agreement.

So, what happens if they are challenged or your manger is replaced with someone less accommodating?

Surprisingly you may well have a case if you are challenged over your informal, flexible arrangement. If the flexible work pattern has been in place for an extended period of time and the arrangement has been consistent you could rightly assert that this has become a contractual arrangement even though your contract has not been amended. You may need to provide evidence that you have been adopting this work pattern for some time to be able to claim that reverting back to your standard hours would result in a change to your working conditions.

Such ad hoc arrangements are likely to become less common. Employers are becoming increasingly aware of the ambiguity surrounding such agreements and are tightening up their systems. The advice seems to be that any arrangement needs to be put down in writing and agreed by both parties to avoid any future dispute.

The reluctant flexible worker

Flexible working certainly doesn't suit everyone. If you find yourself in the position of being forced to change your working arrangements against your will it is a serious matter. The first step is to check your current contract of employment. UK employment law states that the contract of employment can only be changed by mutual agreement. So, if flexible working is not part of your contract of employment and yet your employer is offering you this option, you have the right to either refuse or accept the proposal. However, sometimes life is not so simple. Employers have been known to try and force changes by dismissing staff, usually due to some major change in the organization, and then re-employ them under a new contract of employment. All situations are different but refusal to work flexibly is not grounds for dismissal and if you feel you are being treated unfairly it is advisable to seek legal advice.

Your rights as an employed part-time worker

Part-time arrangements can cover several working patterns but as far as legal rights are concerned a part-time worker is defined as someone in employment who is working less than the full-time hours stipulated for the current role. This includes all those working part-time, job share or any other flexible arrangement that results in working reduced hours.

The Part-Time Workers Regulation, which came into force on 1 July 2000, is designed to ensure that part-time workers are treated no less favourably in their employment conditions than comparable full-timers. This means that part-time employees must receive (pro rata where appropriate) the same treatment as comparable full-timers. The regulation states that this will include no less favourable:

- rates of pay (including overtime pay, once they have worked more than the normal full-time hours)
- access to pension schemes and pension scheme benefits
- access to training and career development
- holiday entitlement
- entitlement to career break schemes, contractual sick pay, contractual maternity and parental pay
- treatment in the selection criteria for promotion and transfer, and for redundancy.

If you are working part-time and believe your conditions of employment to be less favourable than a full-time comparable worker you will need to gather proof. The first step is to identify a comparable full-timer who is receiving more favourable treatment than you. This is not always so easy to do; to qualify, the full-time employee must:

- work for the same employer as you
- do the same or similar work as you
- have a similar level of experience and skills to you where this is relevant to the role.

Having identified a comparable full-time worker, if you still believe that your treatment infringes the Regulation, you have the right to request a written statement outlining the reasons for the inequality. You should submit your request in writing, and your employer is obliged to reply, in writing, within 21 days.

If you are still not satisfied you can make a complaint to an Employment Tribunal. If your complaint is found to be valid, the Tribunal may require your employer to pay you compensation.

TIP: The Regulation also provides protection if you are returning to a part-time role having previously worked the comparable full-time position. In this case you will be able to compare your part-time conditions with your previous full-time contract. This is accepted as a valid comparison as long as you have not had a period of absence of more than 12 months.

Your rights to retirement

Retirement is a hot topic at the moment. The government and employers are waking up to the fact that our mature workforce has a lot to offer, even after retirement age. At the moment when you reach State Pension age (which is 60 for a woman and 65 for a man) you have three choices:

- retire and claim your State Pension
- claim your State Pension while you carry on working
- delay claiming your State Pension.

Currently, if you delay claiming your State Pension you will get around 7.5% extra on top of your pension for every year that you delay taking up your State Pension.

But things are set to change. Legislation regarding retirement is split between the DTI and the Department for Work and Pensions (DWP) and at the time of writing the DTI has been tasked with implementing an EU directive to outlaw discrimination based on age by the end of 2006.

The DWP is working towards the same goals. A green paper published in December 2002 outlines plans to provide a better deal for people who choose to draw their State Pension beyond their State Pension age. The aim is to give you more choice about when you retire. At the moment, you can only put off claiming your State Pension for five years, but this is set to change allowing you to put off claiming for as long as you like. The paper has recommended that the reward for deferring the state pension should be raised to 10.4% from the current 7.5%.

Alternatively, you will also have the option to take a taxable lump sum instead of an increased weekly State Pension. So for example, if you delay taking up your State Pension for at least 12 consecutive months when you do finally claim it, you will get a lump sum based on the State Pension you've delayed plus interest.

As well as the changes to pension deferral the green paper also recommends that:

- compulsory retirement ages are made unlawful, unless employers can show that they are objectively justified
- people should be allowed to continue working for the same employers while drawing their occupational pension
- the earliest age that a pension may be taken should be raised from age 50 to age 55.

Parliament will have to agree to the changes before they can become law. If the changes are approved, they are likely to be introduced in April 2005. For further details on the current legislation and the proposed changes access the DWP's Pension Service website at www.thepensionservice.gov.uk/.

Your rights as a non-employee

Legislation to protect workers from the unscrupulous employer has always been high on the agenda whereas the rights of the temporary worker have been less regulated. This is set to change with regulations already in place to ensure equality for those working a fixed contract; temporary workers may soon enjoy similar protection.

Your rights as a fixed-term worker

The Fixed-Term Employees (Prevention of Less Favourable Treatment) Regulations came into force on 1 October 2002. The Regulations are designed to ensure that 'fixed-term employees are not treated less favourably than comparable permanent employees on the grounds they are fixed-term employees, unless this is objectively justified'.

The Regulations apply to all workers who are employed on a contract that meets one of the following criteria:

- it is scheduled for a specified period of time
- it will end when a specified task has been completed
- it will end when a specified event does or does not happen.

Fixed-contracts are often used to cover for maternity leave or for fixed length projects such as IT developments. In some cases this type of contract is also used to manage peaks and troughs in demand.

Equality for pay and conditions

If you are working a fixed-contract and believe that your conditions of employment are not comparable to a permanent employee carrying out the same role you will need to make a case. The first step is to identify a permanent employee who is employed by the same employer and is doing the same or broadly similar work to you. Where relevant, both you and the comparative employee should have similar skills and qualifications. It is acceptable to make a comparison with a similar permanent employee working for the same employer at a different location.

Having located and identified a comparable permanent employee it is a case of comparing their terms and conditions of employment with your own. If there is a discrepancy you are within your rights to ask your employer for a written statement setting out the reasons for less favourable treatment. You should make this request in writing and your employer is legally obliged to respond, in writing, within 21 days. If you are still unhappy with the outcome you have the right to present your case to an employment tribunal.

Successive contracts

The government is keen to discourage employers from employing a worker on successive fixed-contracts rather than providing permanent status. As a result, the Regulation states that 'the use of successive fixed-term contracts will be limited to four years, unless the use of further fixed-term contracts is justified on objective grounds'. However, it is still possible for employers and employees to increase or decrease this period or agree a different way to limit the use of successive fixed-term contracts via collective or workforce agreements.

There is no limit to the length of the first fixed-term contract, but if a contract of four years or more is renewed, it should then be treated as permanent. If you find yourself in this position you have the right to ask your employer for a written statement confirming that your contract is now permanent or setting out objective reasons why they have extended the fixed-term contract beyond the four-year period. The employer must provide this statement within 21 days.

Other regulations introduced in 2002

1 It is now illegal to include a redundancy waiver within a fixed-contract. Any such waver included in a contract that is agreed, extended or renewed after 1 October 2002 is invalid.

2 Fixed-term employees should receive information on any permanent vacancies available within their organization.

3 The end of a task contract that expires when a specific task has been completed or a specific event does or does not happen will be a dismissal in law. The non-renewal of a fixed-term contract concluded for a specified period of time was already a dismissal in law prior to October 2002. Employees

on these task contracts of one year or more will have a right to a written statement of reasons for this dismissal and the right not to be unfairly dismissed. If the contract lasts two years or more and the contract is not renewed by reason of redundancy, the employee will have a right to a statutory redundancy payment.

4 Employees on fixed-term contracts of three months or less now have a right to statutory sick pay.

5 Employees on fixed-term contracts of three months or less now have the right to receive and duty to give a week's notice after one month's continuous service. These new notice requirements only apply if the contract is terminated before it is due to expire.

Points 4 and 5 put these fixed-term employees on the same footing as permanent staff and fixed-term employees on longer contracts.

Your rights as a temporary worker

At the time of writing your rights as a temporary worker are not on a par with those working on a fixed-term contract. However, this is likely to change if a new European Directive is adopted within the UK.

European Directive for agency workers

The EC has proposed that 'agency workers should not have less favourable employment conditions than permanent workers in the client company where they are sent to work unless this is objectively justified'. This proposal is not extended to posts of less than 6 weeks, or to situations where agency workers are covered by collective agreements or are employed on permanent contracts.

At this stage it is not clear whether the proposal will become a legally binding directive, as discussions are still taking place between the European Council, Parliament and other interested parties. If the proposal does become a directive a transposition date will be set providing enough time for the appropriate legislation to be passed.

The government agrees that temporary agency workers do deserve adequate protection and have ensured that there are specific provisions to cover them within the national minimum wage and working time legislations. However, there are real concerns that the proposed directive could work to the detriment of the temporary worker. By insisting that they are given equal rights to permanent workers, they will become less attractive to some employers, which will have the knock on effect of less jobs being available.

The government is facing tough opposition from professional bodies within the IT industry as well as from recruitment agencies. There are concerns that the plan to give temporary staff the same benefits as permanent staff will damage UK competitiveness as well as affecting the work opportunities of the 1 million temporary workers registered on any given day in the UK.

There is growing speculation that if the Directive is adopted there will be adjustments to the wording to accommodate these concerns. It has been suggested that contract staff may be excluded from the legislation or that the Directive will only apply where a contract of employment or employment relationship exists between a contractor and an agency. The contractor choosing to opt out of the Employment Agency Regulations can easily negate this relationship. But at the moment this is simply speculation.

Current rights

Not everyone is against the Directive. The Trades Union Congress (TUC) has highlighted the plight of the UK's 1.7 million temporary workers stating that almost half of them are paid less than permanent staff. There are also concerns that temporary workers miss out on a range of benefits, such as equal pay and pensions with many not having access to sick leave or holiday pay.

Maternity rights

As a female temporary worker you may qualify for maternity benefits, but you are not entitled to maternity leave. If you are working on a temporary contract and find that you are pregnant there is no obligation for the company that you are working for to give you 26 weeks' statutory leave and keep the job open for you.

If you are an agency worker and paid through the payroll, you should qualify for statutory maternity pay (SMP) from your agency. You must have earned more than the lower weekly earnings limit and have been working for the same agency for 26 weeks by the 15th week before your baby is due and have sufficient national insurance (NI) contributions. You will then be entitled to 26 weeks' SMP. For the first six weeks this will be at 90% of your average earnings and then a flat rate payment for the remaining 20 weeks. For further details access the DWP website at www.dwp.gov.uk/lifeevent/benefits/statutory_maternity _pay.asp#what.

If you do not qualify for statutory maternity pay you may still be able to claim maternity allowance (MA) from the Department for Work and Pensions (DWP). If you are employed or self-employed and have been earning a certain minimum weekly average you will be eligible. The latest you can start claiming MA is from the day after the date your baby is born. You will receive the standard weekly rate or 90% of your average gross weekly earnings if this is less than the standard rate for up to 26 weeks. For further information on MA access the Job Centre website at www.jobcentreplus.gov.uk/cms.asp? Page=/Home/Customers/WorkingAgeBenefits/498#howmuch. The site also provides an application form that you can download.

TIP: You are legally obliged to inform both your agency and the company where you are working that you are pregnant. You should do this in writing as soon as you are aware of your condition so that health and safety considerations are met. This information cannot legally be used as a reason for dismissal.

Pay, pensions and sick pay

Temporary staff are not currently entitled to the same pay or pension conditions as those working on a permanent basis although this may change if the European Directive is adopted.

All workers are entitled to statutory sick pay (SSP) if they have been contributing towards national insurance and have been sick for at least four days in a row including weekends and bank holidays. However, the statutory rates will be paltry in comparison to the full pay that some organizations offer to permanent staff.

Your rights as a freelancer

As a freelancer you have very few rights compared with permanent employees and those working on defined fixed contracts. Freelancers often work for several employers at the same time, some on a regular basis, some occasionally with some assignments being one-offs. Regardless of your circumstances, some recent directives from Europe defining the minimum wage and the number of hours you can legally work are applicable. There are also some universal rights that you should be aware of (see next section) but generally as a freelancer you are responsible for looking after your own self interests and are quite within your rights to insist that your obligations and the obligations of the employer are defined, in writing.

If working as a freelancer you have probably already come across the dreaded contract. Freelancers are usually obliged to enter into a contract to protect both the employer and themselves. Such contracts can take many forms from the simple document stating the obligations of both parties to undecipherable documents full of legal jargon. In the case of the latter it is always advisable to seek the services of an expert before signing.

TIP: It is worth investigating whether your trade or profession provides any expert help in the form of a trade union or society. For example, for those who write for a living, the Society of Authors provides expert help and advice on legal contracts, free of charge for members (www.societyofauthors.org).

Apart from employment regulations there is also additional legislation that can affect the freelance worker, in particular the Copyright Designs and Patents Act 1988. This Act refers to the moral rights of an author and states that an individual has the right:

- to be identified as the author of a work
- not to suffer derogatory treatment of a work
- not to have works falsely attributed to another.

Contracts have been known to include the clause 'waives all of his moral rights' which, in effect, negates all those rights stated above, so be careful what you sign.

Universal rights

1 Every worker, including those who work on a temporary basis or on a fixed-term contract, are entitled to 20 days' paid holiday leave (including bank holidays) each year. Your employer is responsible for paying the holiday wage. If you work for an agency, the agency is considered to be your employer, not the company that you work for, and you must claim the holiday pay from them.

2 In the past workers could not start earning holiday leave until they had worked for 13 weeks. However, following a European court ruling in 2001, workers now start earning paid leave from day one of their employment. The rule was changed to prevent some employers avoiding paying holiday leave by giving their workers a series of 13-week contracts.

3 All workers must be paid at least the minimum wage.

4 Workers who are required to operate heavy machinery or handle dangerous substances are entitled to proper training wherever this is identified as a legal requirement.

5 Workers must also not be discriminated against because of their race, sex, or a disability.

Summary

The government is committed to work/life balance initiatives as demonstrated by the recent legislation to give carers of young and disabled children the right to request flexible working. There is every indication that flexible working will feature on the agenda of all the major parties during the run up to the 2005 general election, with further legislation likely to extend the right to request flexible working to all employees with caring responsibilities.

The national minimum wage and working time regulations apply to all workers and it is the responsibility of the employer/agency to ensure that the laws are adhered to. In principle these regulations also apply to the self-employed even though they are self-regulated and therefore wholly responsible for their own welfare.

In addition to these two laws, employed workers benefit from legislation to ensure that they are not penalized or discriminated against for working reduced hours. However, until fairly recently, there was little legislation to protect the interests of the contract worker. Directives from Europe have now resulted in those working fixed contracts realizing the same conditions and benefits as their permanent equivalents. Workers engaged on temporary contracts may soon also be covered by similar legislation although recruitment agencies and employers of temporary staff are encouraging the government to consider the consequences of such a ruling. At this time it is thought that the legislation will be adopted but with amendments.

04

working from home

In this chapter you will learn:
- about the advantages and disadvantages of home working
- how to make a case for home working
- about the legal and financial implications
- how to set up and kit out a home office
- about health and safety, and confidentiality and security when working from home

When considering flexible working many of us look to the option of spending at least part of our working week based at home. Raise the subject at any social gathering and you will find that the majority of those present have considered the option but few have taken the plunge. So why is this? A 2004 European survey by the recruiters Monster found that more than three-quarters of Britons favour home working but 60% claim that their companies don't offer it as an option. A recent media article also indicated a growing interest in home working. Apparently, 27 per cent of the UK's 35 million Internet users already work from home with 51% more wishing that they could.

So according to the statistics there are a lot of people out there who would work from home if they could. But is this a true reflection of the situation? If these workers were given the option of home working tomorrow would they jump at the chance or would they waver once they had considered the pros and cons? Home working can certainly be appealing but it does not suit everyone. If you're not sure whether this is the flexible working option for you then read on.

Home working facts

Working from home is far from a new phenomenon. The UK census data shows that in 1901 9% of women and 2% of men worked from home. The predominance of women home workers was due to professions such as dressmaking and laundry services making it possible for women to work within the home while minding the house or caring for family members.

Coming more up to date, the total number of home workers in the UK in spring 2001 was 2.2 million, or about 7.4% of all in employment. Although this is a relatively small percentage of the total, the number of home workers is steadily rising. Since 1997 the number of home workers has increased on average by 13% each year and although the self-employed are still strongly represented their share is decreasing and employees now account for the largest share of the yearly increase.

The increase in the number of employees working from home can be attributed to a number of factors. Government initiatives to raise awareness of flexible working options have certainly helped but it is the recent advances in technology and communication tools that have made it easier to work remotely. The home office can now be a seamless extension of any other place of work, be it a large organization or the office of another home worker.

Is home working for everyone?

Broadly speaking those people who work from home fall into one of three categories; those who choose to work from home, those who need to work from home due to personal circumstances and those who work from home at their employer's request. Depending on which camp you fall into you may judge the pros and cons of this type of working arrangement very differently.

Employees will have different issues and challenges to the self-employed and equally those content with their own company will find it easier to adapt than those who thrive on interaction with colleagues. The following pros and cons are from the perspective of the 'average' home worker, working at home through choice.

TIP: The psychological impact of the various pros and cons of flexible working are looked at in detail in Chapter 5, The flexible working mindset.

The advantages of working from home

Less travel time
A recent report from SusTel found that more than 40% of the home workers surveyed saved between 6 and 10 hours' travelling time per week, 12.9% saved between 11 and 15 hours per week with 10% saving over 16 hours per week. Sounds good in theory but not all this extra time was spent on out of work activities, in fact the statistics show that some home workers spend up to 10 extra hours working each week.

Flexible address
As a home worker you can live where you want rather than being confined to a geographical area within commutable distance of a town or city.

Flexible working hours
The flexibility that home working provides has to be a big plus. You can take time out for the school play, visit the gym during

the cheap rate period or simply go for a walk when the sun is shining. It goes without saying that you have to make this time up later in the day but that is a small price to pay for having the flexibility to plan your working day.

Flexibility for carers

Home working can provide the opportunity for carers to join the workforce. Those who care for children or dependant relatives often find it impossible to work the standard 9 to 5 day. Home working can provide the flexibility they need to work at times that fit around their caring routine.

Flexibility for the disabled

British Labour Force Survey figures show that in 1999 around 78,000 disabled people in Britain were home working which equates to about 5% of the total number of home workers. Although not the answer for all, home working has the potential to offer some disabled people new employment opportunities. This flexible approach to the working location can certainly benefit people whose disability causes fatigue, difficulty in travelling to work or in moving around while at work.

The disadvantages of working from home

Isolation

Being home alone can be depressing for some home workers. Email and a few phone calls cannot compare with a gossip around the coffee machine or a departmental lunch out. For some, however, the isolation of home working can be a bonus; the lack of interruptions and mindless chatter may be a dream come true.

Disruption

Once it is known that you work from home you could well become the local childminder. Early morning panic calls from your office-based friends with a sick child, non-working friends popping round for a quick coffee, the scenarios go on but whether this type of disruption becomes a problem is down to you. A firm but polite no and an explanation that, although at home, you are working should do the trick.

Lack of concentration

Working from home does take a certain amount of willpower. If you are tucked away in an office it is not too bad but if working on the kitchen table faced with the pile of breakfast dishes it is difficult not to be distracted.

Out of sight out of mind

Lack of visibility in the workplace is seen as a major drawback of home working. Home workers often complain that they are at risk of missing out on promotion.

Making a case for home working

Although not every job lends itself to home working many do. If you believe you have a case prepare your argument carefully before you leap in. By being able to counteract negative issues you are more likely to succeed in persuading your employer to give it a try (see Chapter 2 for further advice on requesting a flexible working option).

Reputation

The fact that you are trustworthy, self-motivated and disciplined will go a long way to help your case. If you are not renowned for these qualities it may be time to rethink. A manager is unlikely to allow someone to work out of sight if they cannot be trusted to maintain or improve their current performance.

Trial period

Suggesting a trial period with no obligation on either side may help to smooth the way. By initially working from home one day a week, every other week or possibly for a six-month trial period may prove a good starting point.

Do the legwork

Don't approach your manager with a badly thought out proposal. Do your homework and consider the proposal from your manager's point of view. Anticipate any drawbacks and suggest solutions.

Consider costs

Try to keep additional costs to the minimum. For example if you already have a telephone and broadband connected you could ask your employer to just pay for your business calls. You may want to suggest the Home Computing Initiative (see later in this chapter) as a way of purchasing equipment.

List benefits

Make a list of all the benefits such as the extra time you will have by not travelling, your increased motivation etc.

Consider health and safety

Health and safety could be a sticking point. It may help if you agree to take responsibility for carrying out your own health and safety assessment within the home environment (see Health and Safety later in this chapter).

Making it work

Once you've got the go ahead it is up to you to make it work.

- Communicate regularly with management and colleagues both concerning work and social issues; keep yourself in the loop.
- If something isn't working make the necessary changes immediately.
- Make sure that you do not abuse the privilege.

If you get it right you will not only be improving your own work/life balance, you will also be paving the way for other employees within your organization.

Organizations like Surrey County Council need little persuading when it comes to selling the benefits of home working.

Case study: Surrey County Council

Surrey County Council (SCC) offers a full range of flexible working options, but working from home is becoming increasingly popular with around 800 staff now feeling the benefits.

There are various levels of home working – from taking work home to read overnight through to having the equipment and connections available to make working at home almost the same as being in the office. Caroline Cheales, e-Services Consultant at SCC confirms that home working initiatives have helped to both recruit new staff as well as retain valued employees. Caroline estimates that it costs around £1800 to enable someone to work from home, which can be easily justified when compared with the cost of recruitment and downtime while looking for a suitable replacement.

'Almost any member of staff can apply to be a home worker. Managers decide on an individual basis whether they can support the costs involved, and whether the work is suitable for virtual working. With services being increasingly delivered over the web, the need for people to operate from the office or to work standard office hours is reducing.'

Contracts of employment

Flexible working options are often ad hoc arrangements. This can lead to ambiguity and misunderstandings especially if the individual who has been granting you this flexible arrangement moves on.

If you have a home working arrangement that works for you but is not documented as part of your contract of employment you could loose the privilege without discussion. If you know that the arrangement will not be formalized it may be better not to rock the boat but if your organization is open to home working then it is advisable to seek a change to your contract of employment (see Chapter 3, Your rights as a flexible worker, Contract of employment for flexible workers).

Your employer may choose to impose a clause that states that they can change their mind and reinstate the office as your place of work. Equally you can ask for an option to be included so that you can change your mind. Your circumstances may change and home working may no longer be viable.

TIP: Home working certainly doesn't suit everyone. If you find yourself in the position of being forced to work from home against your will it is a serious matter. The first step is to check your current contract of employment. UK employment law states that the contract of employment can only be changed by mutual agreement. So, if home working is not part of your contract of employment and yet your employer is offering you this flexible option, you have the right to either refuse or accept the proposal to work from home.

Legal and financial implications of working from home

Before going to the costly exercise of setting up a home office it is worth considering the legal and financial implications. You presumably want to work from home to make your life easier so it is important to make sure that you are not heading for stressful disputes with neighbours or unexpected costs that you have not budgeted for.

Planning rules and regulations

On the one hand the government is actively encouraging home working and yet their planning departments appear to discourage it. The current planning regulations that discourage home businesses are based on the premise that workplaces and homes cannot co-exist without conflict. This may well be the case with some small businesses particularly those that have expanded to the extent that they cause a nuisance to neighbours – due to noise, smells or too many clients visiting. However, the majority of home workers tend to be individuals using a spare bedroom to double up as an office. This form of home working is unlikely to cause any concern to other residents and in fact may be welcomed by local neighbour watch schemes.

In practical terms working occasionally from home will not be a concern to the authorities. However, more permanent arrangements may be subject to a number of planning and related issues.

As a rule of thumb, where the business use is clearly secondary to the domestic use, there should not be a problem. Problems can arise however where:

- The home worker employs non-residents to work from their home.
- The home worker carries out activities to the detriment of the neighbours; i.e. inviting excessive numbers of visitors to their home, creating excessive demand for parking spaces, operating noisy machinery.
- The home worker makes structural changes to their home in order to provide a home office.
- The home worker erects outbuildings or extensions to be used for business purposes.
- Radio masts, satellite dishes or other devices are erected on the house or in the garden of the home office

Restrictive covenants

A restrictive covenant can be placed on a property at the time of development restricting its use for business activities. This type of covenant is sometimes placed on new housing estates and developments in order to protect the community from noise, disruption or traffic congestion. It is unlikely that neighbours will call upon this legality if you are simply working from home. However, you could engage difficulties if your working activities involve deliveries or visitors causing traffic congestion.

Business rates

Previous to a test case and subsequent appeal in August 2003 you could have been liable to pay business rates for the part of the home being used as a home office. However, as a result of the judgment on this case you will not be liable for business rates as long as:

- the work space can still be used for domestic use
- you haven't made structural alterations to your property in order to create office space
- you don't employ people to work from your home
- you don't have significant numbers of visitors.

If you do contravene any of the above conditions you may be liable to pay business rates on the part of your house that is being used for business.

Tax issues

For most people, tax is a grey and murky area at the best of times but when working from home it can become even more confusing. Legislation and interpretation is changing all the time and it is always advisable to seek professional advice if you are unsure regarding your tax position.

The employed

If you are working for an employer the Inland Revenue have published an advisory amount up to which employers can pay free of tax and national insurance contributions. This amount can be paid without having to provide any supporting evidence of the costs incurred. This tax exemption is to cover incidental costs such as additional expenses for lighting and heating. In many cases the home worker will incur costs in excess of this amount. In this case the exemption can be increased but the employer must be able to provide supporting evidence that the additional payment is for household expenses incurred through working from home.

TIP: The Inland Revenue website will provide details of any changes to legislation that have tax implications for home workers. Announcements are often made as part of the budget and can be found in the budget report (www.inlandrevenue. gov.uk).

To reduce the complexity of tax arrangements, many organizations opt to pay for work incurred expenses directly.

For example, it is common for an employer to install a telephone line in the home office of the home worker to be used solely for work. The employer will then pay the bill directly, negating the need for an expense claim. In most cases, equipment provided exclusively for work will not incur any tax liabilities. Specifically, computer equipment provided by an employer for home use by an employee or his or her family is not taxable.

Travel is another grey area. If an employee is contractually home-based, payment for necessary trips to the office might be treated as a tax-free expense. If you are in this situation it is worth checking with your local tax office. You can find details of your local Inland Revenue office by selecting the Contact Us option from the Inland Revenue website. Alternatively you can find the telephone number of your local office in your local telephone directory. For employers, the Employer Helpline on 0845 7143143 can provide advice.

The self-employed

If you are just starting out as self-employed in the UK, the first step is to contact the Inland Revenue and HM Customs and Excise. You can notify both departments using the same form, CWF1. This form can be downloaded from the Inland Revenue website (www.inlandrevenue.gov.uk/startingup/register.htm). Alternatively, you can telephone the Newly Self-Employed Helpline on 0845 9154515. This form requires you to provide basic information about your business and is relatively simple to complete. If you need assistance, phone the Helpline and staff will guide you through the process.

Once recorded as self-employed it is your responsibility to keep a detailed record of all your business income and expenditure so that it can be used to calculate your taxable profit at the end of your accounting period. These records should also be kept in case the Tax Inspector queries your tax return.

The self-employed can claim two types of expenses, capital and revenue. Capital expenditure is classified as major business expenditure such as the purchase of business premises, machinery, vehicles and the initial cost of tools. You cannot deduct capital expenditure when calculating taxable profits, but some relief may be due on this type of expenditure in the form of Capital Allowances. For further advice on these allowances contact your local tax office or contact the Self-Employed Contact Centre on 0845 9154655.

In general allowable revenue expenditure relates to those expenses incurred during the day-to-day running of your business. It includes salaries, rent, the lighting and heating of the business premises, running costs of vehicles used in the business, purchase of goods for resale and the cost of replacing tools used in the business.

Non-allowable expenditure is costs such as your own salary, income tax and National Insurance contributions.

Insurance

Working from home can affect your equipment, employer's liability and householder insurances.

You may find that your household policy becomes invalid if you work from home so it is important to tell your insurance provider. In some cases it will just be a case of letting them know the change in status. In fact, some household insurance providers actively welcome the home worker appreciating that the higher levels of occupancy during the day can reduce the risks of break-ins. Other insurance providers may charge an additional premium to extend the cover to include working from home.

Even though your household insurance provider has granted permission for you to work from home it always pays to check your small print. You may find that you need a specialist insurance policy if your standard household insurance does not cover any loss or damage to office equipment or cover public liability insurance. If you are using your car for business you may also find that your motor insurance is invalid. It will pay to check with your insurance provider just in case.

Running a business from home

If you operate a business you have legal obligations to your employees, customers and the general public. You must take out employers' liability insurance to cover all your employees including trainees and contract staff. By law you must have cover of £5 million, although most policies will now automatically provide £10 million cover. You must also exhibit a Certificate of Employers' Liability Insurance at each place of work.

You will also find that legal liability cover is more or less essential, although not required by law. There are two types of cover, public liability and product liability. Public liability covers you against accidents to members of the public or damage to property that occurs as a result of your business activities. It will also cover any related legal costs. Product liability covers you against injury or damage caused by faulty goods. This can be important if you manufacture, repair, install or even retail goods.

Setting up the home office

In an ideal world your home office should be a large airy, light room with its own toilet and refreshment facilities. In reality your home office is more likely to be a desk in the spare room, a reclaimed space under the stairs or a quiet spot where you can set up your laptop. Wherever you choose to work it is important to make sure that the environment is conducive to productivity.

Office alternatives

From a space under the stairs to a loft extension to a shed in the garden, home workers can be an imaginative bunch when it comes to finding the perfect home office. Keeping planning permission in mind, it is worth considering all possible alternatives before kitting out your office.

Custom built office

The April 2003 budget included new legislation allowing employees to charge their entire home working costs to their employer, tax-free. This also includes the cost of their personal office as long as the building is a dedicated working environment. This has seen growing numbers of home-based workers buying the latest dedicated personal offices and locating them in their gardens. Although this sounds like a perfect solution you should always check with your local planning office before you buy. You should also be aware that you will be liable to pay business rates on your office premises as well as the domestic rates on your house.

TIP: If you want to investigate the purchase of a garden office further, searching on the keywords Garden Office using an Internet search facility will provide a wide selection of sites.

Live/work property

A live/work property is designed specifically for dual use, to live in and to work in. There are estimated to be around 2,000 live/work properties in the UK; a small number considering that one in every thirteen homes is now occupied by a home worker.

A few years ago live/work property seemed to have a bright future. Fuelled by the dotcom boom, there was no shortage of self-employed entrepreneurs keen to buy a property that they could work from as well as live in. Estate agents predicted that live/work was the way of the future but the market seems to have lost momentum. One reason for the decline in interest is the confusing planning situation. Some live/work units are 'pre-designated' which means that the owner pays domestic rates on the portion of the property that they live in and business rates on the remaining part. However, many live/work homes are not formally split in this way and it is the responsibility of the owner to negotiate with the local council. This can be time consuming, expensive as well as frustrating and has put off some prospective buyers.

TIP: Would-be buyers of a live/work property also need to consider that business properties attract capital gains tax when sold.

Office address

If image is of the essence you may not want your customers to know that you have a home-based office. Some people get round this by giving their house a name or unit number that gives the impression of an office complex. Unit 5, 10 Birch Lane gives the impression of being an office address but it may also confuse the postman when trying to locate a unit at a mid terrace house on a suburban street. Equally, Equity House, 24 The Avenue could also give the impression of a business premises.

Possibly a simpler option is to take a Post Office (PO) Box number. This service, provided by the Post Office, gives you a box number that substitutes for your house number and street name. An address such as HGF Ltd, PO Box 17, WD5 4RF can look as professional as any multinational and gives no indication that, in fact, the company operates from a one-bed room flat above a shop.

Office checklist

There are a number of vital considerations to be made before you set up your home office. Before opting for the home working option you need to be sure that your home environment will be conducive to concentration and productivity.

Noise

Many workers choose to work from home simply to be able to get on with work without the continuous distractions and interruptions of office life. In reality you may find that the home environment comes with its own concoction of noises to drive you to distraction. Consider whether the external noise from traffic, the garden and neighbours as well as internal noise will disturb your concentration.

Temperature

Working in an attic room may seem an ideal solution but make sure that it isn't too hot in summer and cold in winter. Make sure the room can be well ventilated and heated independently in winter. There is little point heating the entire house if you are only using one room.

TIP: Many local authorities provide grants towards loft insulation (the recommended depth is 250 mm). For further information access the Energy Efficiency website (www.saveenergy. co.uk/gid/) or telephone the Energy Efficiency Helpline on 0845 7277200.

Lighting

It is always a good idea to position your working area so that you get the maximum natural light while minimizing the glare if you are using a VDU. It may also be necessary to install blinds or curtains to block out strong sunlight or use a desk lamp if the natural lighting is poor.

Self check

- Is your working area quiet enough for concentration and conversation? ❏

- Is the temperature of the room comfortable in summer and winter? ❏

- Can you adjust the temperature locally? ❏

- Is the work area free from draughts? ❏

- Do the windows have blinds to block bright sunlight? ❏

- Is there adequate lighting for reading and close work? ❏

- Is the VDU positioned to prevent glare from natural or artificial light? ❏

Kitting out your home office

Once you have selected your spot the next step is kitting out your home office with furniture and the technology required to function. If you are working for an employer you may find that the office equipment is supplied for you or, more commonly with smaller organizations, you are given a set amount of money to purchase office equipment such as desk, chair and storage. By choosing your own furniture you will also be able to source items that fit the surroundings and complement your existing furnishings. If self-employed you may well be setting up your office on a tight budget. If this is the case it is well worth paying a visit to a second-hand office furniture shop where you can pick up everything you need for you home office often at a bargain price.

Ergonomics

Sitting at the kitchen table on a hard wooden chair is not going to do you any good long-term. Disorganized workspaces, combined with poor posture and spending too long in front of a computer can lead to chronic health problems.

Organizing your working space is an important part of setting up the home office. To see examples of the right and wrong ways to arrange a computer workstation, go to the following websites: http://openerg.com/dse/ideal.html and http://openerg.com/dse/horrors.html.

Workstation assessment

Before you start working, take the time to assess your workstation and make any alterations necessary to ensure a safe and healthy environment.

Sitting straight on to your keyboard and screen so that you don't need to twist your body or head is the number one rule when working at a computer. Secondly, make sure that you have a good chair that you can adjust to support your back and head. You will also need to be able to alter the height of the chair so that your arms are positioned correctly.

It is also important to keep the area below your desk free from clutter to provide adequate room for your legs. This will also allow enough space to enable you to routinely stretch your legs to boost circulation. Use a footrest if your feet don't rest flat on the floor after adjusting the seat height.

Self check

- Is your desk big enough to comfortably house your equipment and provide adequate working space? ❑
- Is the desk deep enough to allow you to position your VDU at least 20 inches from your eyes? ❑
- Do you have enough legroom to sit square on to your keyboard and VDU? ❑
- Can you adjust the height of your chair so that your elbows are roughly the same height as the desk? ❑
- Can you place your feel firmly on the floor? ❑
- Is your chair comfortable with armrests and good back support? ❑
- Is your VDU tilted between 5% and 15% off the vertical? ❑
- Can you adjust the brightness and contrast of your VDU? ❑

What equipment do you need?

The equipment you need to work from home will very much depend on the nature of your business. A home-based hairdresser or beautician for example will need all the tools of their trade but they will also probably need an office environment for completing their accounts or producing marketing materials. The majority of home workers do in fact require a traditional office type environment. Statistics show that of the 2.2 million people working from home, 1.8 million of these people could not perform their job without the use of both a computer and telephone.

Office equipment

If you are moving from an office environment to a home environment you will be able to determine your needs quite easily. Whatever you needed in the office you will need at home. It is worth considering which office peripheries you actually do use and those that are superfluous to your needs. There is little point clogging up your office space with anything other than the absolutely necessary.

If you are self-employed or starting a new home-based job, you will need to spend some time considering your requirements. The following self check will provide a starting point.

Self check

The following list of office equipment and consumables is comprehensive and designed to serve as a guide to the range of options. It is unlikely that a home worker will need to source all the listed items.

- Desk that is large enough to house a PC if required ❏
- Fully adjustable chair ❏
- Footrest ❏
- Filing cabinet(s) ❏
- Suspension files ❏
- Desk lamp ❏
- Fan ❏
- Portable heater ❏
- Clock ❏
- Plants ❏
- Pictures ❏
- Comfortable chairs and coffee table for entertaining visitors ❏
- Coat stand ❏
- Coffee/tea making facilities ❏
- Small fridge ❏
- Flip chart or whiteboard (and pens) ❏
- Pin board ❏
- Headed paper ❏
- Compliments slips ❏
- Envelopes ❏
- Printer/photocopier paper ❏
- Business cards ❏
- Company brochures, marketing materials ❏
- Files, folders etc. ❏
- Pens, pencils, ruler, paper clips etc. ❏
- Scissors, stapler and hole punch ❏

Non-computer and communication equipment

There are a number of electrical items that you may need that are not strictly classified as computer or telecoms equipment. The required items will depend on the services you are providing. If you will only use these items occasionally or you cannot justify the cost of the initial purchase you should consider using an external provider such as a printer, post office or library. Alternatively you could hire the equipment if you are only going to need it for a short period of time. Examples of such items include: photocopier, shredder, franking machine, post weighing scales, dictaphone, binding machine, laminator, guillotine and overhead projector.

Computer and telecoms equipment

The range and specification of the information technology (IT) equipment you will need will again depend on your business. The following checklist aims to consider all needs.

Self check

- Computer (system unit) ❑
- Keyboard ❑
- VDU ❑
- Mouse ❑
- Laptop computer ❑
- Printer ❑
- Plotter ❑
- Scanner ❑
- Tape drive ❑
- Software (computer programs) ❑
- Modem (to connect to the Internet) ❑
- Telephone ❑
- Answer phone (or call answer/message service) ❑
- Printer cartridges ❑
- Disks and CDs ❑
- Cables and extension blocks ❑

The Home Computing Initiative

If you need to purchase IT equipment it is worth considering the Home Computing Initiative (HCI) before heading for the high street or trawling the Internet. The HCI was first launched five years ago but it has been slow to take off. However, recent media coverage has raised the profile of the scheme and now organizations are beginning to promote the initiative internally.

The basis of the scheme is for the employer to buy computers in bulk and then lease them to employees over a 3-year period. The scheme also extends to computer peripherals such as printers. The lease payment is then deducted directly from the employee's pay without incurring either income tax or National Insurance contributions. In practice this means that basic rate income tax payers save 22% of the cost of the computer plus an additional 11% through not having to pay the national insurance. Higher rate income tax payers will benefit even more saving 40% on the cost of the computer, plus the NI saving. And, into the bargain, the employer also benefits by not having to pay the employer's NI contribution on the cost of the computer.

On top of the income tax and NI saving, as long as your employer is VAT registered you will also save the VAT amount levied on the computer, which will provide a substantial saving of 17.5% of the overall cost.

Taking this all into consideration by leasing under the HCI you will save:

- an initial discount on the computer due to the bulk purchase
- the income tax levied on your lease payment
- the National Insurance levied on your lease payment
- the VAT levied on the cost of the computer.

This can result in your payments over the three years being less than half the amount you would pay for the same computer model purchased in the high street. And at the end of the 3-year lease period the employee is usually given the option to purchase the computer for a nominal price of around £50. Alternatively you can re-enter the scheme and lease a new model.

To find out more about the HCI take a look at the Department of Trade and Industry (DTI) website, www.dti.gov.uk/hci. You can also request a guidelines pack by telephoning the DTI on 0870 150 2500.

Health and safety for the home worker

Home working throws up new health and safety challenges as people work in places that are not tailor-made for business use. We live in an increasingly litigious world and those responsible for health and safety are quite rightly concerned about the implications.

Statistics indicate that deaths and accidents in the workplace have steadily declined over the years, whereas deaths and accidents in the home are showing a steady increase. If employers are encouraging their staff to work from home they have a responsibility to ensure that they are not putting them into an environment with its own set of risks and dangers.

If you work for an employer, your employer is responsible for your health and safety regardless of where you are working; although it is important to be aware that you also have a duty of care, subject to adequate training and support. This responsibility for health and safety can prove a sticking point when an employee is trying to negotiate a home working arrangement as employers often have concerns regarding the implications of this liability.

The management of Health and Safety at Work Regulations (1999) state that employers are required to carry out a risk assessment of the work activities carried out by a home worker. By carrying out this risk assessment the employer is tasked with identifying any potential hazards and ensuring that steps have been taken to prevent harm coming to the employee or anyone affected by their work.

In the office environment the designated health and safety manager undertakes risk assessments directly. Carrying out risk assessments at individual homes can be intrusive, time consuming and costly. Larger employers tend to find that self-assessment is the best approach, with home workers carrying out their own risk assessment. This is usually backed up by training, support and provision of equipment such as chairs, desks and lighting.

If you are responsible for self-assessment of the health and safety aspects of your home working environment then this should be stated in the terms and conditions of employment. Where this is the case the employer should provide details of how you can carry out a risk assessment and provide assistance and help where required.

Whether you or your employer has legal responsibility for health and safety at your home, it makes sense to keep yourself and your family safe. This also applies if you are self-employed where the onus is completely on you to ensure that your working environment is safe and secure.

TIP: The Health and Safety Executive (HSE) publishes a document entitled *Health and Safety of Homeworkers: Good Practice Case Studies.* For further details access the HSE website (www.hse.gov.uk/research/rrhtm/rr262.htm).

Risk assessment

There are five steps to a risk assessment:

1 Identify the hazards.
2 Determine who might be harmed and how.
3 Assess the risks and take appropriate action to remove them or reduce them as far as possible.
4 Record the findings.
5 Check the risks from time to time and take further steps if needed.

The most common hazards can be summarized as:

- handling loads
- using work equipment at home
- using electrical equipment for work at home
- using substances and materials for work at home
- working with VDUs.

When working from home the risk assessment you make will depend on the nature of your business and the equipment and substances you are dealing with. Within the average home-office the main health and safety areas that you will need to assess can be defined as follows.

Handling loads

Regardless of the situation or location there are simple rules to be obeyed when handling loads. If you are employed you should have received basic manual handling training, otherwise take the time to read the guidelines at the HSE website (www.hse.gov.uk/pubns/indg143.pdf) or phone the Infoline on 08701 545500 to request a copy of the document.

Using work equipment at home

It is important to ensure that you have created an ergonomically sound working environment (see previous section, Ergonomics). Consider the position and brightness of the computer screen, the position of keyboard, lighting levels, furniture and posture. Make sure that the room temperature and ventilation is suitable.

Using electrical equipment for work at home

If you are using electrical equipment that has been provided by your employer it is your employer's responsibility to ensure that the equipment is maintained. If you have supplied the equipment or you are self-employed then the equipment is your responsibility. Irrespective of who has supplied the equipment, you are responsible for the electrical sockets and other parts of the domestic electrical system within your home. Regardless of formal responsibility, it makes sense to ensure that equipment is safe, and that the available sockets and power supply are adequate for the equipment installed. It is also important to ensure that there are no trailing cables that might constitute a danger.

Self check

The following points should be checked when using electrical equipment for work at home:

- Make sure that the domestic electricity supply is adequate for the equipment you intend to use. ❑

- Make sure that plugs are not damaged. ❑

- Make sure that the plugs are wired correctly. ❑

- Make sure that the outer covering of the cable is gripped where it enters the plug and the equipment. ❑

- Check that all cables and wires are free from damage – do not use any cables with splits in the outer covering. ❑

- Check that the outer and protecting coverings of all equipment are secure and undamaged. ❑

- Make sure there are no burn marks or scalding that could indicate that equipment is over-heating. ❑

- Check for trailing wires and cables and make sure that they are secured so as not to cause a hazard. ❑

If you **do** find any faults with the equipment stop using it until the problem has been remedied.

Most of the faults that can constitute a danger can easily be identified by regularly working through a checklist. Produce a list of all your electrical equipment and document the possible faults that may occur. Work through the list on a regular basis, noting any faults. If your employer has provided the equipment you can also use this document to inform them of any problems.

Using substances and materials for work at home

In this instance, a hazardous substance or material can be defined as anything that may cause harm to the home worker, their family or visitors. An employer is only responsible for substances or materials that they provide for the home worker. Anything provided by an employee or a self-employed home worker is their responsibility.

Health and safety risks can arise from the misuse or inadequate storage of hazardous substances. Also, hazards can occur from use or misuse of equipment, such as using a telephone without a headset while typing or operating an industrial sewing machine without gloves. The important thing is to assess the potential hazards and take steps to ensure your own safety and the safety of those who reside in or visit your home.

TIP: Small children and toddlers are skilful at locating all kinds of potential hazards. Office equipment such as scissors, staplers and bottles of screen cleaner can soon become play items. If you ever have children at your home, look at your home office through their eyes. Make sure that anything that could prove hazardous is either out of reach or locked away.

First aid

Employers need to ensure that they supply adequate first aid provisions for home workers. The exact requirements will vary depending on the risks involved with the job. Self-employed home workers are advised to ensure that they have adequate first aid experience to deal with any accidents that may occur in the workplace.

If your first aid knowledge is patchy spend some time working through the interactive online first aid course provided at the BBC website www.bbc.co.uk/health/first_aid_action/.

Reporting, monitoring and follow-up

Employers should not consider health and safety as a one-off concern at the time of set-up. They must ensure that periodic assessments are made and also reassess the situation when new equipment is introduced or the nature or location of the home working is changed.

Employees also have a duty to report and keep a record of work-related accidents, injuries and incidents in the same way as you would if working at your employer's premises.

If offering a home working alternative most organizations will have some method of time recording so that they can monitor compliance with the European Time Directive (see Chapter 3, Your rights as a flexible worker). It is important to appreciate that this recording of working hours is necessary for your own health and safety as well as being a legal requirement.

There are very real risks that home workers will work excessive hours and fail to take necessary breaks, ultimately to the detriment of their health and work quality. Recording the amount of time worked during a daily or weekly period can help you, and your employer, identify when you are putting in too many hours and adjust your workload appropriately. However, if you are self-employed it is down to you to monitor your work/life balance and ensure that you are not heading for burn out.

Home worker personal safety and vulnerability

Personal safety

Depending on what you do, you may find that from time to time you need to meet with clients or suppliers. Meeting at your home may not be a viable option especially if you are self-employed and trying to project an image of a much larger operation. Although home working is gradually becoming more acceptable, for many meeting in the home is still not perceived as professional with home workers preferring to organize an alternative meeting place such as a hotel or serviced office. For others, the relaxed atmosphere of the home environment is conducive to informal business meetings. From a personal safety point of view, however, if you do not know the client meeting at another venue can make sense; inviting a stranger into your home should always be avoided wherever possible.

For those offering a service from home such as training or beauty/medical treatments, meeting clients at home is unavoidable. If your job does require you to work alone and have clients visit you at your home you should protect yourself by taking a few additional precautions.

- Even if the client makes the initial contact, obtain details such as their office/home phone number, website and address. Do not just accept a mobile telephone number.
- Attempt to verify that the information is correct/acceptable and they are in fact who they say they are.
- Always inform a colleague, family member or friend that you are expecting a visitor.
- Provide details of who you are meeting and at what time.
- Ask someone to be present at your home during the visit if you have any doubts.
- If you still feel uncomfortable, cancel the meeting/appointment. Some business is just not worth the risk.

Home worker vulnerability

People looking for home working business ideas can be vulnerable to a number of home working scams. Working from home schemes are often advertised in local and national papers as well as on websites. These schemes often follow the same pattern: there is a PO Box number, no telephone number (or if there is you get an answer machine) and most importantly you have to pay money up front. The advice is if you are at all suspicious don't part with your cash. Although some of these schemes are legitimate many are not. As with all such scams the perpetrators prey on our desire to make lots of money for little effort. If the job seems too good to be true it probably is. If you do decide to give it a go in the UK, it is sensible to check the company name on the Companies House website (www.companies-house.org.uk).

In the UK, there are an estimated 17,000 home workers in a variety of low paid jobs. These jobs often involve packing or assembly and are paid based on the time it takes an average worker to complete a task. From October 2004 employers are required to provide clearer information regarding the rate the employee is expected to work at and the hourly rate of pay. This involves the employer carrying out tests to determine the hourly output rate and setting the rate of pay to comply with the minimum wage rate.

Confidentiality and security

Whether employed or self-employed you have a responsibility for the confidentiality and security of information within your home. Taking work away from the office, either physically or electronically, can increase the risk of confidential information being exposed.

There are a whole range of technological solutions such as virus checkers, passwords, encryption and firewalls that can keep the outside world from hacking into your personal electronic data but these tools are only as good as the person operating the computer. If you do not load and update virus checking software or load firewall software then you cannot ensure that the data is safe. Equally, passwords must be kept secure and confidential information should not be left displayed on the computer screen for other members of the household or visitors to view.

If other members of your family also use the computer you use for work it is important to ensure that they cannot access your work data. It is also essential that you back-up your data as accidents can so easily happen.

Physical data such as confidential papers can easily be stored in lockable drawers and cabinets. When no longer required, paper copies of confidential documents should be shredded rather than deposited in the household dustbin.

Data Protection Act

To quote the European Directive on which the Act is based, the Data Protection Act 1998 is designed 'to protect the fundamental rights and freedoms of natural persons, in particular their right to privacy with respect to the processing of personal data'. The Data Protection Act 1998 has eight principles designed to make sure that information is handled properly.

The data must be:

- fairly and lawfully processed
- processed for limited purposes
- adequate, relevant and not excessive
- accurate
- not kept for longer than is necessary
- processed in line with your rights
- secure
- not transferred to countries without adequate protection.

If you are self-employed and are storing and processing personal data using a computer you may need to register with the Information Commissioner as a data controller. If you are employed to process data, either at home or in an office, it is the responsibility of your employer to register as a data controller. By law, data controllers have a duty to maintain the eight principles detailed above.

Registering as a data controller is known as notification. You, or your employer, need to notify if you are responsible for maintaining and processing personal data using a computer. In this context, personal data is data that relates to living individuals who can be identified from the data; and processing means obtaining, recording or holding the data or carrying out any operation on the data such as organizing, adapting and amending. In real terms it is difficult to think of any activity involving data that cannot be classified as processing.

TIP: If the processing of data does not involve a computer you do not need to register.

Individuals are exempt from notification if the only data they process is for personal, domestic and household use such as a personal address list, Christmas card list or data held in connection with a hobby. Exemption does not apply to individuals who hold personal data for business or professional purposes.

You can check whether you are exempt or whether you need to notify by accessing the Information Commissioner website (www.informationcommissioner.gov.uk). There is a useful self-assessment guide that you can work through online. Alternatively, telephone the Notification Line on 01625 545740.

TIP: Beware of bogus agencies requesting payment for data protection registration. If you believe you have been approached by a bogus organization inform your local Trading Standards Office and do not correspond with the organization or pay any money.

The Telephone Preference Service

The Telephone Preference Service (TPS) was set up to preserve the sanity of individuals being bombarded by unsolicited telephone sales calls. By registering with the service the individual is stating that he/she does not wish to receive sales calls and companies can be fined for ignoring this fact. The question is, if you are self-employed and have been contracted to make sales calls on behalf of a company, who is responsible for making sure the numbers have been checked against the register? The legal response is that it is down to both parties. The company on whose behalf the calls are made as well as the company whose telephone lines are being used to make the calls are both responsible for making sure that calls are not made to numbers registered on the TPS.

Businesses (or those subcontracted by other businesses) who make unsolicited sales and marketing calls to individuals or other businesses need to comply with the regulation. This applies equally to charities and voluntary organizations. It is the responsibility of the business making the call to check both 'cold' lists and customer lists against the Telephone Preference Service File before calls are made. If the individual or business is listed on the TPS File then they should not be called. The only exception is where the subscriber has already indicated to the calling business that they do not object to sales and marketing telephone calls.

You can obtain a list of subscribers registered with the TPS by completing an online application form and returning it to the TPS office. There are a number of different options available for accessing the data and you will be invoiced depending on your choice.

To find out more about TPS and the fee structures for accessing the data, visit their website at www.tpsonline.org.uk/tps/ or telephone the Subscriptions Department of the TPS on 020 7291 3326.

Summary

Working from home has both advantages and disadvantages but for many the flexibility it brings far outweighs any negative aspects.

Before setting up a home office you need to consider whether the environment is conducive to home working and whether there are any legal implications with working from your home. There are also the practicalities to consider such as acquiring appropriate furniture and equipment, taking health and safety implications into consideration.

Chapters 7 and 8 consider the technologies that have opened up home working to the masses. The Internet and related communication technologies have enabled office-based staff to re-create their working environment in their own homes. The evolution of the seamless office has endless opportunities. In this chapter we have looked at home working but as you will see in Chapter 9, working from home is just one of the many remote working possibilities.

05 the flexible working mindset

In this chapter you will learn:
- how to manage family expectations
- how to manage yourself
- how to recognize the challenges faced by your manager
- how to manage the expectations of colleagues
- how to manage the expectations of clients

In later chapters we will look at technology that can help you to work anytime anywhere, but of course having the right technology is only part of the battle. Psychological and social pressures can also play a significant part in your ability to work flexibly, particularly if you opt to work alone on a permanent rather than occasional basis. Feelings of isolation, guilt and being 'out of sight, out of mind' can have a negative impact on your ability to succeed and turn what might otherwise be a liberating experience into a prison sentence. This chapter is about developing the right mindset to cope with new ways of working, and to make the most of the opportunities that flexible working can bring.

Managing family expectations

It is clear from recent studies that a significant proportion of the working population would like to work more flexibly. In fact, according to one recent survey, British employees would prefer to work better hours than win the lottery!

For many, flexible working represents the perfect opportunity to spend less time travelling to work and more time with the family. In one study, statistics show that working from home appeals to a greater proportion of people with dependants (39%) than to those with no dependants (24%). However, although a desirable solution for many, working from home can have its drawbacks. Both you and your family will really need to be on top of your game from the outset if you are going to make a success of it in the long term.

Contrary to expectations, many flexible workers end up working longer hours in an effort to prove that they can work reliably and productively from home. In the process they find themselves increasingly alienated from friends and family. Where once work and home life were clearly defined – get up at 7 am, dress in a suit, leave the house, go to the office, work with colleagues, leave for home at 5.30 pm, relax with the family for the evening – the boundaries between the two can suddenly become blurred. Work is no longer something intangible that you do away from home; it is something visible and real, something that affects every member of the family.

Working from home or working flexibly is likely to mean significant changes for everyone around you. You need to be prepared for the fact that some members of your family may adapt to it better than others. This section is relevant for anyone taking on a new flexible working role and who needs to gain the support of friends and family to make it work.

Reaching an understanding

At the end of the day it doesn't really matter what flexible working means to you as an individual. What matters is making sure that you and your family understand and agree what it means for you as a unit. When you reach an understanding it is important to establish a routine as quickly as possible and determine to stick to it.

To prevent difficulties arising there are a number of strategies and skills that you can develop. Communication is at the heart of them. In principle, if you follow the steps below and keep revisiting them on a regular basis you won't go far wrong.

- **Plan and communicate** – work together to draw up an outline of what flexible working will mean for the family as a unit.
- **Anticipate and prepare** – highlight potential problem areas and agree a plan of action that will address tricky situations before they arise.
- **Act** – stick rigidly to your agreed working schedule until you and your family become comfortable with the routine.
- **Evaluate** – set a regular time aside to discuss how things are going. Agree to try out a new approach where a current one is failing.

Both yourself and your partner should complete the following self check separately.

How do you think working flexibly would benefit you and your family? Here are some commonly cited reasons. Add more if necessary.

What will flexible working mean for your partner and children?

- Less time travelling and more time spent with family. ❏
- Savings in terms of petrol and parking costs. ❏
- Ability to cover childcare without outside help. ❏
- Opportunity to share daily chores. ❏
- Emergency cover if one of the children is sent home from school ill ❏

What will flexible working mean for you?

- Opportunity to see more of children. ❏
- Opportunity to go cycling/walking in the park etc. when the weather is nice. ❏
- Less stress and more energy due to reduced travelling time. ❏

What are the potential benefits to your company?

- Greater creativity and productivity as it will be easier to concentrate at home than when working in a large office. ❏
- Hot-desking will save the company money. ❏

When you and your partner have completed your self checks, number the points in each section in order of importance to you. Now sit down with your partner and discuss the points that you have both made under each section. Did you list the same benefits or are there any discrepancies? For example, was your partner surprised to find that you are hoping to take some time out for yourself during the working day? What about order of priority for each point? Are some things higher up the list for your partner than yourself?

Now list potential problem areas and agree what you can do to minimize conflict. Here are some examples:

Potential problem area

The children may want me to play with them when I need to work.

What is the best way of dealing with it?

- Explain to the children why you have decided to work flexibly and what the benefits will be to you as a family. Your family will appreciate the fact that part of the reason you have chosen to do this is so that you can spend more time with them.
- Once you have talked about the benefits it is important to point out that these changes are likely to impact on your daily routine and this is something that you will all have to try and get used to.
- In order to prevent any conflict creeping in later on it would be a good idea to set ground rules together from the start.

Potential problem area

I would like to be able to go for a cycle ride during the day but I'm worried that my partner may resent this 'time out'. I will also feel guilty taking time out during the day.

What is the best way of dealing with it?

You could suggest one of the following:

- You and your partner take time out to go for a cycle ride together.
- Your partner has some quality 'me' time while you look after the children/do chores.
- You go for a cycle ride early in the morning before everyone else is up etc.

Potential problem area

I would like to take on a greater proportion of the daily chores but I'm worried that this will encroach on my working time.

What is the best way of dealing with it?

You could suggest one of the following:

- You do your share of the daily chores before you start work in the morning or during your lunch break.

- You tell your partner that although you will be unable to take time out to do shopping during the working day, you will take on the task of sorting household affairs that require form filling or contact by phone etc.

In managing family expectations:

- Keep things in perspective and try to be realistic about what you can hope to achieve in the short term.
- Don't be too hard on yourself. Be prepared for things to go wrong in the early days – there are bound to be issues that come up along the way.
- Encourage an open dialogue.
- Don't let problems escalate – deal with issues as they arise.
- Recognize that there will always be a solution. The difficulty will be in finding a solution which suits everyone, but it will be worth the effort in the long run.

Setting ground rules

It is important to start as you mean to go on. Now that you have an idea of potential problem areas, let members of the family know how important your work is to you and what your priorities are. Agree realistic ground rules so that everybody knows what to expect and how to contribute to a successful outcome. Work together to manage the changes. Conflict is likely to arise if:

- rules and boundaries are unclear
- family members have different expectations of the situation
- communication is poor.

Consider the following areas of your working life and agree a way forward.

Hours of work

When you are working from home more often, friends and family may see your time as more accessible, particularly if they have few constraints on their own time.

Self check

- Decide on a set of core working hours when you will
  need to concentrate on work and will be generally
  unavailable. ❏

- Decide on a set of times when you will be available
  to chat, play, take the dog for a walk, put the
  washing in etc. ❏

- Let everyone around you know what your core
  working hours are to be and stick to them. People
  will soon get used to being told that you need
  to work. ❏

Roles and responsibilities
It is important to be clear about your new role in the family
unit.

Self check

Will you be able to:

- take the children to school and pick them up
  again at the end of the day? ❏
- take friends and family to appointments (dentist,
  doctors etc.) during the day? ❏
- walk the dog? ❏
- provide cover in the case of emergencies? ❏
- do household chores? ❏
- do other tasks that may deviate from your
  working day? ❏

It may be expected that with more time at home you can do all
of the tasks listed in the self check. Avoid conflict by deciding
what you can realistically expect to contribute without resulting
in too much additional stress to yourself.

Dealing with interruptions
Decide how you will let your family know if you are hard at
work and not to be interrupted. For example, let everyone know
that if your office door is shut it means that you need to work

quietly and without interruption. Explain that this is because you need to have peace and quiet to be able to concentrate and shutting the door will help you to work better.

Give reasons when it might be particularly important not to be interrupted. For example, it would be nice not to have a few little faces appear alongside yours on the screen when you are talking to a client via webcam. Let everyone know that if the office door is open then this is a sign that it is fine to come in.

Exercise
Try this traffic-light system with your family as an alternative way to help you deal with interruptions. Use three coloured pieces of card (or similar) for your office door:

- Red time – time when you should not be disturbed, unless there is an urgent task or emergency.
- Amber time – time when you can be disturbed but would prefer not to be.
- Green time – time when you can be disturbed.

Think about how you will handle the situation if your red time is interrupted. And, just as importantly, how will you positively reinforce the importance of 'red time' to others around you?

Dealing with phone calls
Phone calls from friends, colleagues and clients can prove very stressful if you haven't decided how to handle them in advance.

Self check

Have you decided how you will hande a phone call if:

- it is from a friend phoning to have a chat during your working hours? ❑
- you are elsewhere in the house when the phone rings? ❑
- you have someone with you when the phone rings? ❑
- you need to go out for a while? ❑
- clients and colleagues call when your family are at home? ❑
- clients and colleagues call out of hours? ❑

Here are some potential strategies:

- If you are too busy to talk to friends during working hours then be honest and tell them so or try to keep calls short.
- If you are going to be otherwise engaged or away from your desk, get into the habit of putting the answer machine on, diverting the phone to another landline or mobile and leaving a sign on your messaging program to say that you are temporarily out of the office.
- Ask friends and family not to pick up the phone during the day or, alternatively, install a separate line for business calls and keep the house line free for personal calls.
- If a business contact is likely to call to speak to you during the evening then prepare a script so that other people know how to answer the phone. For example: 'Hello. No I'm sorry X is not here. Can I take a message for him/her? If you leave me your name and telephone number I'll tell him/her that you have called.'

If you don't think about these things in advance, you may find yourself trying to 'shoo' people away while you try to concentrate on what the caller wants from you or risk losing calls when you are away from your desk.

Managing your office space

If your office is currently a general purpose space, other members of the family may take it for granted that they can come in at any time and play games on the PC or do homework, etc. If at all possible, set aside a separate working area or office. It will pay dividends in the end.

Self check

Have you decided:

- who can use the PC in your office and when? ❏
- what you will do with your papers at the end of the working day? ❏
- where you will store and secure confidential information? ❏

Here are some things that you can try if you do get interrupted:

• Agree how much time the person will need from you and try to stick to that.
• Keep checking your watch to show that this time is valuable to you.
• Keep the other person standing.
• Keep the conversation on track and summarize the points as a way of drawing the conversation to a close.

Managing yourself

If you have come from a working environment where you have been used to being managed by others you may find the switch to independence difficult. Flexible workers often feel isolated and worry about being 'out of sight out of mind'.

Self check

Do you worry that:

• you will miss out on work-related social activities? ❑
• your colleagues and manager will think that you are not pulling your weight? ❑
• your contribution to the team will go unrecognized? ❑
• you will be passed over for promotion? ❑
• you will be first out of the door if the company decide to make redundancies? ❑
• you will be kept in the dark when it comes to changes in company strategy and general company information. ❑

If you identify with these concerns, it may be that you have been previously employed or are still employed by a company that fosters a culture of 'presenteeism'. That is where being present at work is seen to equate to productivity. However, whatever your experiences, you are not alone. These feelings are normal and fairly typical of the flexible working population. Moreover, they are relatively easy to overcome.

Case study: SUSTEL

SUSTEL (Sustainable Teleworking) is a 2-year research project on teleworking carried out on behalf of the European Commission's IST (Information Society Technologies) initiative. Its findings showed that 24% of survey participants felt they had lower career prospects. However, on the positive side, 80% of those surveyed also reported lower stress levels.

In order to feel in control you need to develop a range of skills. In addition to being determined and confident, you will need to be:

- a good communicator
- self-disciplined
- motivated
- organized.

The good communicator

Communication skills are vitally important, whatever your line of work, but they are particularly important to the flexible worker. As a flexible worker you might find that the opportunity for face-to-face meetings is limited, in which case you will need to become a more effective communicator by phone or email. Even if you are particularly good at organizing regular face-to-face meetings, you may need to fine-tune your meeting skills so that you receive and get across the information you need in the time that you have allowed.

Face-to-face meetings

Face-to-face meetings can be an important lifeline for the flexible worker. They are a chance to keep in touch and feel a part of the wider world of work. It is important to make an effort to schedule regular meetings with clients, your manager and or work colleagues.

Ad hoc meetings

Never underestimate what can be gained from informal meetings. Calling in at the office every now and again will not only remind people that you are part of the team, but it will also give you the chance to discuss ideas on an informal basis. In a traditional office you will nearly always find someone around to bounce ideas off or to clarify your understanding of a situation.

Self check

To get the most out of meetings ensure that you do the following:

- Before you attend a meeting make sure you have read and understood the agenda. ❏

- Prepare in advance what you are going to cover and decide how you will get your points across. ❏

- Before you leave the meeting, check your understanding. You might not get another chance. ❏

Questioning skills

Questioning skills form a vital part of all meetings. You will need to develop a range of skills depending upon the purpose of the meeting, your audience, and the type of information that you want to elicit. Use open questions if you want to encourage debate or a more comprehensive answer than just a simple 'yes' or 'no' response. Open questions are framed using 'how', 'where', 'when', 'what', 'who' and 'why'.

Listening skills

Listening skills are equally vital and can be much more difficult to achieve than questioning skills. You can indicate that you are actively listening through:

- your body language – using engaging facial expressions, establishing eye contact, nodding, sitting forward
- summarizing
- taking notes.

Self check

Do you:

- after speaking take time to pause and wait for a response?   ❏
- look out for non-verbal signals which indicate that a person is waiting to speak?   ❏
- respect the fact that others have a right to contribute? ❏

Communicating at a distance

Communicating at a distance requires a different skill set from that required in face-to-face communications. For example if you are working remotely and have to rely on email or telephone to communicate with the outside world, much of the usual non-verbal element of communication evident in face-to-face meetings will be absent (e.g. eye contact, posture, facial expressions) and research has shown that non-verbal cues can play a much greater part in the communication process than verbal cues.

Case study: Non-verbal cues

Some research carried out in 1972 showed that people were five times more likely to believe non-verbal cues than what was being said. For example, if a hostile message was delivered in a friendly way, people were more likely to ignore the antagonistic words and believe that the deliverer's intention was friendly.

The case study research and other research demonstrate the power of non-verbal signals. As a result if you want to become a more effective communicator over distance you may need to work on developing your verbal skills as well as a much narrower range of non-verbal communication skills to compensate for this fact.

By telephone

When you talk over the telephone, be aware that the person at the other end may 'read' more into your conversation than you intend. They may pick up on the fact that you are under par or struggling to cope with your workload. You need to be particularly aware of communicating non-verbal signals if you regularly 'hand over' to other colleagues over the phone, as often happens with people who job share.

Case study: Speech patterns

Research carried out in 1965 showed that colleagues can judge your emotional state by tuning into the rate and volume at which you speak as well as listening to your rhythm, pitch and inflection. If you are angry or anxious, for instance, you will tend to stutter, repeat yourself and make more mistakes. Similarly, if you are unsure of your subject matter or unsure of the person to whom you are speaking, you are more likely to punctuate your sentences with lots of 'ums' and 'ers'.

The message is simple. Although you may spend a lot of time thinking about what to say, people are equally likely to take note of your tone of voice and other paralanguage clues.

Self check

Before you begin a phone call, do you make sure that you are:

- in a positive and cheerful frame of mind?   ❑
- calm?   ❑
- sure of your subject matter?   ❑
- sure of what you want to say?   ❑

Self-discipline and the work/life balance

If you have a tendency to be a workaholic or a perfectionist, you may be tempted to prove your worth by working additional hours over and above those you are contracted for. Not only that, but if your office is at home, the temptation to work will be easier to satisfy. Be warned. Working long and unsociable hours can be a slippery road to disaster. Not only can you disenfranchise friends and family, but you can also end up tired, stressed and feeling increasingly dissatisfied with your new lifestyle.

However, as with everything in life, flexible working is about striking the right balance. Working additional hours works well for some people, and only you know whether you are alienating family and friends by working overtime. Perhaps you will feel that the benefits of putting in extra hours far outweigh the negatives.

Case study: Dawn

Dawn France is a Resourcing Consultant for HBOS retail. HBOS retail currently employs in the region of 44,000 people and Dawn's job involves recruiting new staff to the business.

Dawn is an enthusiastic exponent of flexible working. At the moment she works a 9-day fortnight with 2 days per week spent at her desk in Halifax. The rest of the time she is out visiting clients and prospective employees. She organizes her days off around the needs of the business.

'I love my job and the flexibility that I get from it. I manage my own diary, which means that I am free to make appointments and travel around the country to see clients as and when I need. One day I might be in Scotland and the next in London.

'When I first approached HBOS to do flexible working it was because I wanted study leave. When my studies ended I felt guilty going for a walk on my days off instead. Now, though, I don't feel guilty any longer. I frequently work more than my contracted hours (which I am very happy to do) and I never claim overtime. So, if I've worked some very long days in a particular week, I don't feel guilty about lying in bed the next morning or doing a bit of shopping in between appointments. I'm happy to do as many hours as necessary to meet the needs of the business in order to have the freedom to organize my working life.'

Keeping the number of hours worked in balance

Most office or factory-based workers work a set number of hours each day with clear start and finish times. With flexible working it may be much more difficult to get into an established routine.

In the short term, you can stick to a routine that you are familiar with. Do you:

- work traditional office hours from home? ❏

- set core hours that you will work and stick rigidly to, whatever your workload? ❏

- appreciate that 'more' does not mean 'better'? (Don't be tempted to burn the midnight oil or work weekends to finish off projects that are on your task list. If you are an employee, your manager will want to have a realistic appreciation of what you can achieve in the time set and you should be honest and upfront if you are struggling to get through your workload. Although you may impress your manager with your short-term productivity, you will fail to impress if you end up taking time off in the longer term through stress-related illnesses.) ❏

- listen to your body? (Frequent headaches, eye strain, palpitations and disturbed sleep can all be signs of stress. Don't ignore them. Stop what you are doing and rest.) ❏

Motivation

Keeping motivated will be one of your main challenges, especially if you have been used to being motivated by other people around you or have responded well to employer-reward systems. As an independent worker you may have to draw strength from your own internal resources if you want to stay motivated.

Be organized and disciplined

If you are an employee with a designated line manager, work with your manager to:

- Create a realistic set of goals and objectives. If not, work out your own task schedule based on what you have to achieve.
- Keep focusing on achieving your targets throughout each week.
- Regularly review your progress. Are you meeting your goals? If not, why not? If something isn't working, change it.

Exercise some flexibility

- If you cannot get your head around a particular task, do something different for a while and come back to the task later on.

Be positive

- Don't give in to negative feelings like guilt, failure or inadequacy. They serve no purpose. On the contrary, tell yourself how good you are and how well you are doing!

- A problem shared is a problem halved, or so the saying goes. If you have a problem with a task that you think you cannot sort out alone, talk it through with someone else (friend, family, colleague, manager). It's amazing how tackling a problem successfully can boost your self-confidence.

Minimize isolation

- Increase contact with colleagues by arranging social events, days out to discuss work, lunch meetings and conferences.

- Build like-minded contacts through local business associations etc.

- Keep contact with your manager so that you can both be sure of your progress, workload, deadlines and performance. Communicate via email, meet via video conferencing and arrange regular meetings.

- If there is nobody at home all day and you find it too lonely and quiet at times plan calls, meetings and other outside contact.

- Don't suffer from cabin fever (using the same building as home and office all day) – plan regular work and non-work outings. Exercise is important, even if it just means taking a walk to the post box.

- If you have concerns about career progression and how you are performing in relation to others, ask for feedback. Have informal counselling sessions.

Recognize what motivates you

- If you are the type of person who needs regular contact with others, build this into your working day. Call the office at pre-set times, meet a friend for lunch, take a regular gym class.

- If you need to work in an orderly environment, make sure you get your desk and office organized before you start.

- Respect your bio-rhythms – work when your energy levels are high.

- Have a strategy for tackling tasks – e.g. do them in order of priority, do the least appealing tasks first etc.

Create a reward system
- Do something nice for yourself – go for a walk, meet a friend for lunch, read a magazine.
- Take regular breaks. It is important from a health and safety point of view to make sure that you have regular breaks away from a computer screen and desk. Work out a system that suits you best, for example, every half an hour for 5 minutes, every 2 hours for 15 minutes.
- Finish early if you have completed a special piece of work.

Organization

If you are currently employed on a flexible basis, make sure that you are prepared for working away from the office on specified days.

Self check

Check that you can answer the following questions satisfactorily:

- Do you have all the documents and files that you will need to work on? You don't want to keep enlisting the help of colleagues to provide missing information. ❑

- Do you need a copy of work files on CD, disc or paper? ❑

- How will you send and receive information? Will you need to use a fax machine, photocopier, PC, scanner, and if so, do you have access to these tools? ❑

- Have you told the appropriate people how, when, where and under what circumstances you can be contacted? ❑

- Have you agreed when or how frequently you should call into the office? ❑

- Have you agreed how your telephone calls should be handled while you are out of the office? ❑

- Have you agreed who to contact in order to keep in touch with what is happening in the office and who to inform of your progress? ❑

The flexible working manager

If you currently work for an employer and want to work more flexibly, there is no getting away from the fact that your line manager is probably going to be one of the most influential people in helping you make it happen. Whether you feel able to request alternative working arrangements in the first place and, indeed, whether your requests are subsequently granted are both likely to be influenced by the personal attributes of the manager to whom you report. Ultimately, your success as a flexible worker is also likely to depend on the relationship you have with your manager and his or her skill at managing you from a distance.

The significance of the manager

With the best will in the world and the most expensive technology to hand, you may still struggle in your quest to work flexibly without the support and skill of a good line manager. Research carried out in this area shows that managers can play a significant role in the success or downfall of the flexible working role within a company. More traditional managers who feel out of their comfort zone are perhaps most likely to undervalue the skills and role of the flexible worker, and this can have all sorts of repercussions for you as an individual and for the organization as a whole.

Case study: Flexible working options

A conference board survey of 155 companies revealed that while around two-thirds of them offered flexible working options, less than 1% of staff took it up. The reasons given included the fact that their managers didn't trust people to be productive when unsupervised.

Source: *Investors Business Daily*, 28 June 1994.

Family-oriented employment policies

An increasing number of organizations have developed family-oriented employment policies. Typically these make provision for employees to apply for a permanent flexible working arrangement as well as providing the option to work flexibly during periods of personal stress. However, there is a great deal of variation between organizations both in the nature of the policies that they have developed and in the way in which policy information is disseminated throughout the organization. This can have a huge impact on the way an individual manager will deal with requests for flexible working and translate a policy into practice.

Case study: Line managers

There has been some fascinating research in this area. A study carried out in 2003 on behalf of the Joseph Rowntree Foundation for its *Work and Family Life Programme* analysed over 100 interviews of line managers across a variety of organizations and industry sectors. Managers were both male and female and came from a range of age and background experiences. They also included those with and without parental or carer responsibility.

The analysis showed that while some managers clearly understood company policy on flexible working and how to implement it, many relied on a subjective interpretation of the request for flexible working.

There was also a great deal of variation in the level of discretion that managers felt they had in making a decision about whether a request should be granted and the kinds of arrangements they felt able to make. For example, some managers made stereotypical judgements based on gender about the kind of employee who would be likely to request flexible working arrangements. Some also made a judgement about the employee's level of commitment based on whether they were willing to work longer hours than contracted for.

Organizational factors were often key influencers in a manager's decision to grant flexible working arrangements. Such factors included the size of the organization, the ability to arrange cover for the employee, hours of operation, skills needed to run the business and whether or not the employee had a customer-facing role.

Many managers also expressed concerns about the lack of training they were given in this area. In particular, they felt a pressure to respond to employee needs while needing to meet challenging business objectives. However, where managers had received training they were seen to have a greater awareness of company policy and commitment to its delivery.

Case study: Human Resources

An Industrial Society survey of over 500 HR professionals found that over 90% worked in organizations that provided some form of flexible working. However, rather than having clear, visible, formal policies on flexible working, one-third of those surveyed operated flexible working practices on an informal level.

What makes a good remote manager?

In actual fact, the skills required for a remote manager are not significantly different from those of a traditional manager. The main difference is that the worker is not always visible. Unfortunately, some managers couple this lack of visibility with less accountability, dedication and commitment to the job than office-based counterparts.

Managers working in a traditional office environment have the advantage of evaluating a worker's performance through a range of informal and formal means. They can:

- Observe the employee directly at work.
- Check understanding on a regular basis through formal meetings.
- Meet in situ and on an ad hoc basis as necessary.
- Receive informal and valuable feedback from a worker's colleagues.

By contrast, the less visible flexible worker is more likely to have their progress assessed in terms of quantifiable output rather than quality of work. If you have a manager who feels uncomfortable managing people from a distance, it may be down to you to arrange regular meetings or, at the very least, to keep your manager informed of progress by phone or email.

Managerial skills

If you want to work flexibly but have not yet been assigned a manager, you can use this section as a guide to help you to decide who within the company would have the right skills to manage you. If you already have a manager, reading this section will help you to work together to create a successful framework for flexible working.

A skilled remote manager will:

- Assess the characteristics and limitations of the worker and make an informed decision as to whether flexible working is a suitable option for both the individual and the company.
- Be aware that even though a person may be largely suited to flexible working, there may be aspects of their working life which require input from a wider team. For example, a creative writer may need the peace and quiet that comes from working from home but may also need to take part in regular brainstorming sessions to stimulate creative thoughts. If a project is particularly complex, he or she may also benefit from having the opportunity to meet informally or formally with other people so that they can get a holistic perspective of the project.
- Create clear lines of communication between the flexible worker and the office.
- Be approachable and encourage open dialogue, mutual trust and cooperation.
- Take time to get to know each individual employee and their personal circumstances.
- Work remotely themselves from time to time so that they understand the feelings and issues involved.
- Be a 'champion' for flexible working within the company. Talk positively about the value of achieving a better work/life balance and be proactive in promoting and implementing company-wide flexible working strategies.
- Work with the flexible worker to agree a set of objectives and goals.
- Devise a plan to help the worker meet their targets and set deadlines.
- Review progress against targets and give regular constructive feedback.
- Recognize that individual productivity levels may be higher than average but contribution to teamwork may be lower.
- Consider smarter ways of working that will help to support the business and meet the needs of both the flexible worker and office-based teams. For example, where it is no longer feasible for a flexible worker to carry out part of their current role (such as a customer-facing role), the manager may look at innovative ways of meeting the business needs. This may involve redefining specific business processes or offering the role to an office-based worker.

- Keep the flexible worker involved in the company and encourage positive team dynamics.
- Make sure that flexible workers receive regular information bulletins about procedural or strategic changes, client updates and social events and facilitate regular business and social meetings and put processes in place to make sure that flexible workers are invited to attend as a matter of routine.
- Celebrate the successes of the flexible worker in much the same way that the successes of an office-based worker would be celebrated.
- Recognize the important contribution that flexible workers make to the development of the whole organization. A significant proportion of flexible workers are senior managers and, given the right opportunity, they can play an important role in mentoring younger employees.
- Encourage flexible workers to take responsibility for managing their working life.
- Ensure that flexible workers receive appropriate training and career counselling opportunities.
- Make sure that adequate technical support is provided – office-based workers experiencing a temporary equipment glitch will usually be able to find a replacement or share resources fairly quickly; home workers may not be so fortunate.

Case study: Alan 1

Alan McAvan is head of Retail Employer Relations for HBOS in the UK. Alan has worked for HBOS for many years. During the time that Alan has been with the company he has seen a gradual evolution from standard working hours to more flexible working patterns. Flexible workers are now highly valued at HBOS and Alan is proud to work for a company that gives people a tremendous range of working options.

Alan currently manages a team of seven people who each have their own flexible working arrangement. Alan was asked how he manages people under these circumstances:

'I place a high premium on trust and communication. The more you give to people, the more you get back. The people I work with almost universally work more than their contracted hours but they balance this against the huge control and flexibility they have over when and how they work. It works exceedingly well.'

Flexible worker managers

Ironically, although some traditional managers are reluctant to manage flexible workers, they are often ideally placed to work from home or on the move for part of their working week. If you are considering managing remote or flexible workers it would be a good idea to experience the issues they face first-hand.

Case study: Alan 2

In addition to managing a flexible working team, Alan McAvan also works from home when he needs to get some quiet work time. Working from home has helped him to understand the issues that his team face:

'In spite of HBOS's positive and supportive attitude towards flexible workers I still find it difficult to break out of the traditional working mould. I still feel guilty when I work from home and, consequently, I rarely take a lunch break. I find this really strange because I nearly always take a lunch break if I'm working in the office. And although I love to work to music I don't allow myself to play music during the working day whereas, if I'm catching up with work at the weekend I have no qualms about putting a CD on!'

Do you have the attributes that a manager will look for?

If you are in the early stages of making a decision about flexible working, it is a good idea to know in advance what characteristics and skills your manager is likely to appreciate. Use the following checklist to assess your current position.

the flexible working mindset

Self check

Are you:

- able to work autonomously and make decisions without relying on appreciation or consent from others? ❏

- able to work in isolation? If you are usually the hub of the office social scene your manager may think that you will not enjoy working alone for long periods of time. ❏

- able to organize your own time and work space? ❏

- self-determining and well-motivated? ❏

- able to create a home set-up which is conducive to remote working? ❏

- a long-standing employee or someone who colleagues will feel able to call if they need advice? ❏

- mature, responsible and trustworthy? ❏

- demonstrating a healthy professional respect for the company? ❏

If the answers to some of the above are 'no', give yourself a period of time to improve those areas and create the right impression.

Case study: Phil

Phil Glanfield is the Director of the Performance Development Team at the National Health Service (NHS) Modernization Agency. The team provides customized support to zero star (or 'failing') NHS Trusts. Its aim is to help the trusts to make sustainable improvements in key performance areas such as clinical governance, access and waiting times in both elective and emergency care.

The team is multidisciplinary and drawn from a wide variety of NHS and other backgrounds. It is made up of doctors, nurses, executive directors, risk managers, admin staff and patient consultants, to name but a few. Most of the team members have other roles outside of the development team. For example, associate general practitioners (GPs) work primarily as GPs. 90% of staff work from home either on a permanent or part-time basis.

The team could not function without flexibility. Phil believes that its success is down to a number of factors:

- a supportive top-down culture
- the skills, experience and motivation of team members who are focused on making a valuable contribution while maintaining a work/life balance
- the roll-out of mobile technologies.

Managing the expectations of colleagues

Just as you may need the support of a good manager when you work flexibly, you also need to have the support and goodwill of colleagues around you. If you work for a company where flexible workers are viewed with distrust, then you may have to work extremely hard to prove your commitment to those around you. If, on the other hand, you work in an organization where flexible working is the norm, you are more likely to find teams of people that pull together.

Case study: Surrey County Council

Surrey County Council's Workstyle project is a huge flexible working initiative in the UK. The aim of the project was to free staff from the restrictions of when, how and where they worked so that they could better service the needs of their customers.

'Almost any member of staff can apply to be a home worker,' says Caroline Cheales, e-Services Consultant at Surrey County Council. 'Managers decide on an individual basis whether they can support the costs involved, and whether the work is suitable for virtual working. With services increasingly delivered over the web, the need for people to be "at the office" or to work "office hours" is reducing.'

In addition to the technological challenges, one of the biggest challenges facing the project team was to implement cultural change. Team communications became central to success as people began to work from other locations across the county and were frequently offsite. A more flexible approach to meetings and general communications had to be developed to support changes in the business.

Managers too faced a learning curve. They needed to consider a variety of different options for keeping in touch including face-to-face meetings, team briefings, using IT tools and informal get-togethers. And they had to start assessing an individual's contribution based on output rather than the number of hours worked. Teams were coached and supported through the changes at every stage.

The benefits of these cultural changes have been numerous. Working alongside colleagues from other services has given staff a wider appreciation of the work that the organization does as a whole. The changes in managerial style have also led people to feel more appreciated by their managers.

Self check

Trust is one of the biggest issues facing you as a flexible worker. Your colleagues are more likely to trust you if you follow certain procedures. Do you:

- keep in regular contact both by phone and by dropping in to the office? ❑

- arrange regular meetings and social events? ❑

- make sure that your colleagues know where you are, what hours you are working, whether you are contactable and how to contact you? Make sure they also know how to respond to client enquiries etc. on your behalf. ❑

- agree how to handle calls to both your home and the office? (for information on telephone answering services see Chapter 8, Communication tools) ❑

- keep colleagues informed of your work schedule and progress? ❑

- form part of the team and celebrate successes? ❑

- make sure that workloads are equitably and fairly distributed between you and your office-based equivalents? For example, colleagues may resent it if you seem to have all the interesting work and none of the tedious work to do, as well as having the flexibility to do it when you want. ❏

- appreciate other people? It is important not to take others for granted. If you rely on your office-based colleagues for help or information, try to keep your requests to a minimum. If you do receive help, make sure you show your appreciation. It doesn't take long for resentment to build up, especially when people feel that you are taking advantage of their goodwill. ❏

- show sensitivity and openness to the views of your colleagues? If you do, you or your manager can anticipate problems and knock them on the head before they happen. ❏

- make sure that other people don't feel put upon or forced to take on part of your previous office-based role without consultation? For example, you may no longer be able to do a customer-facing role. ❏

Managing the expectations of clients

Your clients may be internal or external, depending on the nature of your job and this may affect how you manage their expectations when you are working flexibly. Your approach will also depend to some extent on how comfortable you are with a particular client and whether they too work for an organization where flexible working is supported. Before making any announcements to clients, discuss how you should handle this issue with your manager.

Contact details

If you are an independent worker and are worried that it will appear unprofessional if clients realize that you are working from home, honesty is probably the best policy. Let clients know that you spend at least part of your working week working from an office at home and that you are contactable via phone and email during your working hours. As long as they can contact you without too much trouble, most clients will be more than happy with this arrangement.

Where to meet

The question of whether you would bring a client to your home is very much down to you and how well you know the person. Think carefully about the following:

- There may be personal security issues with bringing someone into your home. Have you considered all the issues? Take into account the number of times that you have met the client before, the length of time that you've known them, the amount of information you know about them, for example, name, company name, department, email address, landline number, mobile number etc.
- How will it look from a professional point of view? Do you have enough space to hold a business meeting? Is your house tidy?
- How you will dress for the meeting?

If you would consider running a meeting from home, it's best to be upfront with the client so that they know what to expect.

Case study: Lynn

Lynn is a single parent who has been running a business for the past 15 years. She normally works out of a large office in the city centre but occasionally works from home.

'I have a lot of clients that I've known for many years. Recently I had a big meeting arranged for a day when unfortunately my son was sent home from school ill. Although I wouldn't normally consider running the meeting from home, on this occasion I knew the client well and decided to be completely honest about my situation. The client was fine. In fact, the meeting went really well. We were able to get through a lot more items without the usual disruptions in the office.

Before the client arrived I made sure that the house was tidy and that I had enough coffee and biscuits in the cupboard. I also dressed in my suit, after all, it was a business meeting like any other. I don't think I would contemplate doing this with everyone though!'

Summary

Now that you know how to manage the expectations of family, colleagues and clients, the next chapter will concentrate on the skills you need to effectively manage your time. Without these skills you may find it difficult to achieve the work/life balance that you aspire to.

06 managing your time

In this chapter you will learn:
- how to view time as a resource
- about planning
- about self-discipline and personal effectiveness
- how to work with your manager

This chapter is primarily aimed at people working away from the traditional office environment, rather than at those employed on a flexible time basis but spending most of their time working from an employer site.

With the frenetic pace of life today, it's easy to understand why many of us complain that there are just too few hours in the day. On top of work, we have to find time to shop, garden, do DIY, keep fit, organize holidays, socialize with friends and so on. At times it can all seem a little overwhelming. Managing time becomes an issue for most of us at some time in our working lives but it is a particularly fundamental issue for the flexible worker who needs to be self-sufficient, disciplined and organized right from the outset.

If, like many people, you regularly find yourself struggling to balance your work and domestic life, you will need to be prepared to put in a lot of hard work to change the way you manage your time. Old habits die hard and it will be especially difficult if you have been used to having your time organized for you or you have worked (or still work) for an organization where being physically present at work and putting in long hours is perceived to be related to hard work and commitment. However, there is no doubt that learning to manage your time effectively is going to be one of the most important and rewarding skills you will ever need to develop.

Exercise

Take a moment to reflect on how well you feel you manage your time at the moment. Complete the following questionnaire by ticking the appropriate boxes.

	Mostly	Sometimes	Seldom
1 Do you enjoy your working day?			
2 Do you enjoy your free time?			
3 Do you feel satisfied with the way you spend your time?			
4 Are you giving your family as much time as you would like?			
5 Do you have time for a hobby?			

	Mostly	Sometimes	Seldom
6 Do you feel stressed about the number of things that you have to do in a day?			
7 Do you feel obliged to do lots of things that you don't want to do?			
8 Do you take work home in the evenings?			
9 Do you work during the weekend?			
10 Do you work longer hours than you would like?			
11 Do you feel that you could manage your time better?			
12 Do you feel that you always need to be doing something productive?			

If you have answered 'Mostly' to Questions 1–4 and 'Seldom' to Questions 5–12 it is probable that you are managing your time pretty well. However, if the balance of your answers is largely the other way around, you need to take a good hard look at how you are spending your time. The next exercise will help you to do this.

Exercise

List three benefits that you would get from managing your time a little better. If appropriate, list three ways in which your employer might benefit.

For example, it would be useful to your colleagues if you created a work schedule; it would help them to be aware of your objectives and timescales.

Time as a resource

To be an effective time manager, you need to see time as a resource that you have at your disposal, a resource that you can use wisely or that you can squander. How you use time is likely to make all the difference to the satisfaction you get out of your new working life. Use it wisely and you will feel in control of your working day and feel free to enjoy your leisure time. Squander it and you may feel destabilized and out of control.

In brief, in order to make good use of your time you need to:

- be aware of the time that you have available
- know what you need to achieve over that period of time
- plan your time accordingly.

If you are new to flexible working it will be all too easy to muddle through with only a vague idea of the time you have available to you and a partially formed plan of how you are going to achieve your objectives. Yet the fact is that even if you get the work done on time, other parts of your life are liable to suffer. Pressure can build up to the point where it puts a strain on relationships and your health. Start as you mean to go on. Have a clear understanding of the time you have available and create an action plan that demonstrates how you will meet your objectives. And most importantly, stick to it.

Quantify time

If you know that there are 168 hours in 7 days, you can allocate 40 of these hours to work and still have 128 hours to spend as you please. Similarly, if you set aside 160 hours for work over a month, you should have 512 hours to do as you please.

If you have to do something by the end of the week or month, work out the number of hours that you have available to complete the task in the period running up to the deadline, and schedule your time accordingly.

Planning

Knowing how much time you have is only half the battle. The danger is that without careful planning and self-discipline you will work longer hours than intended and your work life will begin to encroach on your leisure time. A survey of over 1,200 workers in the US, Australia and Europe revealed that:

- only 5% worked a standard working week
- 29% worked up to 5 hours more than contracted for
- 57% worked an extra 6–20 hours per week
- 6% worked more than 20 additional hours per week.

If you suspect that, like the workers in the survey, you will be one of the 95% who work more hours than necessary, you need to take a good hard look at how you are spending your time at present and understand why you spend your time in this way. Most importantly, you need to be prepared to make critical changes in the way you view and plan your activities.

Exercise

Keep a daily diary of activities over the next 3 days. Fill in a table similar to the one below showing what you did in each of the half-hour time slots.

Monday		
Time	**Activities**	**Essential**
9.00 am–9.30 am		
9.30 am–10.00 am		
10.00 am–10.30 am		
10.30 am–11.00 am		
11.00 am–11.30 am		
11.30 am–12.00 pm		
12.00 pm–12.30 pm		
12.30 pm–1.00 pm		
1.30 pm–2.00 pm		
2.00 pm–2.30 pm		
2.30 pm–3.00 pm		
3.00 pm–3.30 pm		
3.30 pm–4.00 pm		
4.00 pm–4.30 pm		
4.30 pm–5.00 pm		
5.00 pm–5.30 pm		
After 5.30 pm		

Now go through each of the activities and tick those that were essential.

1 Add up the number of hours spent on essential tasks each day.
2 Total the number of hours spent on essential tasks over the 3 days.
3 Add up the number of hours spent on non-essential tasks each day.
4 Total the number of hours spent on non-essential tasks over the 3-day period.
5 What proportion of your time has been spent doing essential as opposed to non-essential tasks?

Goals and objectives

You can only really know which tasks are essential if you have a clear idea of your objectives. At any one time you should know what you are hoping to achieve in the long-term and be able to translate these goals into medium and short-term objectives. For example:

Long-term goal
To write a quarterly health and safety report

Medium-term objectives
- Attend monthly meetings of the health and safety executive.
- Record and investigate all accidents within 12 hours of being notified.
- Visit six sites to carry out health and safety checks.
- Review two safety websites each month.

Short-term objectives

Date	Goal: to write following sections by end of week
Monday 15 November	Introduction
Tuesday 16 November	Accident reports
Wednesday 17 November	Safety improvements for accident sites
Thursday 18 November	New legislation
Friday 19 November	New European initiatives

When you write your objectives, make sure that they are SMART:

- Specific
- Measurable
- Achievable
- Realistic
- Time-based.

Exercise

1 Write down what you need to achieve in the coming month/quarter.

2 Now make a list of all the things that you have to do over the coming week.

3 Now answer these questions:

a Are there items in your weekly task list that are not related to your long-term goals?

b Are there items in your long-term goals that do not appear in shortened form in your weekly task list?

c Ask yourself whether your long-term goals are clear. If not, seek the advice of family, friends, colleagues or your line manager and make sure that you are on track.

d Ask yourself whether each of the tasks on the weekly task list is necessary. Will they help you to reach your long-term goals or are they a red herring?

Although it is entirely possible that there will be long-term goals that do not feature in your current weekly task list, or indeed weekly tasks that are in addition to your long-term goals, it is a good idea to carefully review one against the other on a regular basis. It can be all too easy to fall into the trap of investing time in tasks that will bring little benefit in the long run, especially if the tasks are ones that you enjoy doing.

Prioritize

To plan your time effectively you need to decide the order of priority for each of the tasks in your schedule. Without adopting a logical approach you are more likely to tackle activities that are within your comfort zone and succumb to mounting pressures as important deadlines loom.

Exercise

1 Once you have decided what tasks should be in your list, place each task in one of the boxes in the table below:

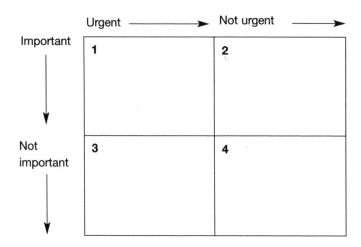

In order to spend your time wisely it is important to keep your attention focused on the activities that are most important – the ones that help you to achieve your objectives. Work through your activities in the following order:

Box 1 Important and urgent
Box 2 Important but not urgent
Box 3 Urgent but not important
Box 4 Neither important nor urgent

2 Take a look at your list again and separate your activities into one of the following three categories:

Must do	Should do	Nice to do

Now work through those tasks that you must do, followed by those that you should do and finally, if you have time, those that would be nice to do.

Planning and recording

Having the right systems in place to manage your work schedule is an important part of the process. This will also help you to justify your progress to clients or to your manager!

There are a variety of options open to you for recording information. It doesn't matter whether you decide to use a paper-based system or a more sophisticated computerized system. The important thing is to choose something that works for you and makes it easy for you to keep up to date.

Paper-based system

If you prefer to work on paper, decide what information you want to record and create a daily 'To do' list based on the categories. See the example below.

'To do' list

'To do' lists are a useful mechanism for making sure that things do not get forgotten. If used properly, they will give you an overview of your workload and help you to see which tasks can be delegated to others:

Task	Date to be completed by	Priority	Status	Further action
Call Peter Stephenson re: project quote	Friday 19 November	High	Not started	
Place stationery order	Wednesday 17 November	Low	Not started	Order printer cartridge
Send Toni email re: Guy's requirements	Monday 15 November	High	Done	None
Send contact list to Sam	Tuesday 16 November	Medium	50% completed	Complete list

Although having a 'To do' list is better than having no list at all, it is still important to try and prioritize the items on the list so that you can complete the most urgent and essential items in time. Work from, review and update the list at the beginning of each day.

Diary

A diary can be used as a daily or weekly planner and, along with a 'To do' list, can provide all the structure you need for a successful working day. Most people use diaries as a way of booking appointments. The fact that your diary is free of appointments on a particular day, however, does not mean that your time is free of commitments. Use your diary to schedule all demands on your time, including those where you are unavailable to meet because you have other pieces of work to do. Silly though it may sound, if you are used to having someone else manage your diary in the office, you may need to get into the habit of checking your own diary each morning.

A diary can be more useful than a 'To do' list because it enables you to plan your time in chunks throughout the day and the week. Work through your list and try to group activities so that you are dealing with similar tasks at the same time. For example, you could set aside the first hour of every morning to make phone calls or respond to emails.

Electronic planners and PC software

Where possible, use electronic planners or PC software to create your work plans. Computer programs will enable you to create and organize task lists in such as way that you can easily update the information, and changes will take immediate effect. There are a whole variety of personal organizers on the market that are specifically designed for this purpose. As with all computer programs, planners vary in price and functionality; so before you make a choice think carefully about what information you need to record. Make sure that you will be able to record and retrieve information that will be sufficient for your purposes.

Computer calendars

Computer programs often have a calendar facility to help you plan your time. If you have a PC with the Microsoft suite of products, you will probably have Microsoft Outlook or Outlook Express as one of your email programs. Outlook has a task list that you can work from each day. Software programs such as Outlook provide additional functionality over and above using a paper-based system. You can insert details such as:

- the task subject
- task due date
- task start date
- task completion date
- total number of hours worked
- mileage and billing information
- status (in progress, completed, waiting on someone, deferred etc.)

You can also set a reminder so that you don't forget to do the task and you can even assign the task to another person. In addition, the software allows you to:

- move tasks around the list
- view all active tasks
- view those due to be completed in the next 7 days
- view those that are overdue.

Word-processing tables

Word-processing packages can be used to help scheduling. If you have Microsoft Word, you can create a 'To do' list using tables. Although Word is not specifically designed for scheduling tasks it does have features that will make it easy for you to manage your list. For example, tasks that are created in table format can be easily moved within the list and deleted.

Task	Date to be completed by	Priority	Status	Further action
Call Peter Stephenson re: project quote	Friday 19 November	High	Not started	
Place stationery order	Wednesday 17 November	Low	Not started	Order printer cartridge

Use the drop down 'Table' menu to create a table. Each task is entered as a row in the table. You can delete a row by selecting it and then selecting the 'Table' menu followed by 'Delete', 'Row'. You can move a row to another position by selecting the row and then holding down the Alt and Shift keys together while you press the Up or Down arrow key.

Spreadsheet planning

Spreadsheet computer packages can also be used to create tables for work scheduling. You may feel more comfortable using a spreadsheet program than a word processing program and so you could create your task list using a package like Microsoft Excel. Information can be entered into the cells on the spreadsheet and then easily moved and deleted.

Self check

Find out whether you are planning your tasks well. Do you:

- set aside half an hour at the beginning of the week to schedule your tasks for the week? ❏

- prepare a list of things that you must achieve for the next day at the end of each working day? ❏

- write your plan in order of priority and work through it systematically? ❏

- plan your time in chunks – grouping common tasks together where possible? ❏

- allow a portion of time for 'general tasks'? ❏

- review your plan at lunchtime and re-prioritize your tasks if necessary? ❏

- accept the fact that things will change and this is an important reason for planning, not a good excuse to avoid planning altogether? ❏

- remember that it doesn't matter what system you choose provided that it works for you? ❏

- stick to your chosen system? If you find that you are duplicating information in several places, your system is not working as well as it could. Change it! ❏

Self-discipline and personal effectiveness

You can have the best tools at your disposal but still fail to manage your time effectively. The most important part of the mix is you. In this section we give guidelines on how to make sure you are working effectively.

Distraction techniques

Distraction techniques are activities that take your focus away from the all-important work that you need to be doing. If you are already a flexible worker you will be familiar with a whole host of techniques that you use and the excuses that you make to yourself along the way. Complete the self check to see which of the more typical ones you might be using:

Self check

Do you identify with any of the following?

- I can't work without having a cup of coffee in the morning.   ❑

- I need to put the washing in so that I can concentrate on work.   ❑

- If I go to the bank now, it will save me rushing at the end of the day.   ❑

- I need to put a CD on as background music but I have to find one that is conducive to working.   ❑

The list of distraction techniques is endless. And it doesn't really matter what is on the list. All items have one thing in common – they are designed to put off that fateful moment when you need to start work!

Exercise

Be honest with yourself and make a list of the distraction techniques that you use on a regular basis. Also make a note of when you are most likely to use them, how much time they take up, and how you feel about using them.

Distraction techniques	When used	Time taken	How do they make you feel?

How to deal with distractions

Dealing with distractions will take a great deal of self-discipline. After all, by their very nature they are so much more attractive than the job in hand. You can deal with distraction techniques in the following way:

- **Step 1** – the first step to success is to accept the fact that you are unlikely to do away with distractions altogether.
- **Step 2** – given the above, the second step is to look at them in a positive light and accept the fact that you can use them to good purpose. For example, taking a coffee break can give you a well-deserved breathing space and time to think through an important issue.

Look at the distraction techniques that you use on a regular basis and ask yourself:

- Why do you use them when you do?
- How important are they to you and why?

For instance, if you put washing in the washing machine at mid-morning each day you may have made a conscious decision to do this because it will give you a chance to get clothes dry for the next day. In addition to this being a useful chore to have out of the way, you know that it should only take 5 minutes out of your working day and therefore it's not really worth worrying about.

Time wasters

Concentrate on eliminating distraction techniques that seem to have little purpose and that increase your frustration levels. For instance, the increased isolation of working from home can make checking emails, communicating with people via Instant Messenger, phoning people or surfing the net, an appealing set of distractions. Although enjoyable pastimes, and necessary at times, if you find that these activities are eating into your working day, the only way to deal with them effectively is to remove them from temptation:

- Ask friends not to contact you during the working day.
- Check your emails at set intervals throughout the day and then immediately close the program down.
- Set yourself the target of only using an Instant Messaging program when needed for work during the day.
- Surf the Internet before your working day begins.

Allocate time for distractions

When you have eliminated unnecessary distractions and are left with a list of those that you feel improve the quality of your working day in some way, try to set a specific time to carry these out. For example, if you can get them all out of the way in one go, say at the beginning of the day, set yourself a limited time period and start to work through them. If you have not completed them within the allotted time, be strict with yourself and stop!

For those distractions that don't naturally fit into an allotted time, try using them as a reward by dividing your day into set periods – say 1.5 hours – and allowing yourself to break up the day with a distraction technique on the list. For example, tell yourself that if you work through until 10.30 am you can have a cup of coffee or if you work through until lunchtime you can do the washing up or surf the Internet.

Behavioural and work patterns

Having an understanding of the types and number of distraction techniques that you use will provide you with a useful insight into the way you operate as a person. You may be extremely self-disciplined and find that you use few, if any, distraction techniques during work time. On the other hand, you may find yourself subjected to constant interruptions and not know how to handle things for the best.

It's not particularly useful to compare yourself to others. The important thing is to have an understanding of the way *you* function as a person and how this impacts on your working life. You can then employ a range of strategies to help you improve specific areas of your working life so that you become more efficient and productive.

Exercise

You can tell a lot about your patterns of behaviour by asking yourself a few simple questions. For example, with which of the following statements would you strongly agree?

Statement	Strongly agree
I frequently alter my priorities and this affects how much I get done in a week.	
I am easily distracted.	
I tend to do the things I like first	
I often miss my deadlines.	
I can't work unless I feel creative.	
I find it difficult to say 'No'.	
I always answer my telephone, even if it rings during an important face-to-face conversation.	
I tend to put off doing things that are unpleasant.	
I usually start my day by having a coffee, a chat or reading the newspaper.	
I often feel guilty about all the things that I'm not getting done.	
I seem to jump around from task to task and often leave things unfinished.	
I often take work home in the evenings because I don't have enough time to complete it at work.	
Things often take longer than I anticipate.	
I find myself doing other people's work because I don't trust them to get it right.	
I regularly analyse my systems to see if they can be improved in any way.	
I know what my short-, medium- and long-term objectives are.	
I use a follow-up system to help keep track of outstanding work.	
I create a task list for each day.	
I always prioritize my tasks.	
I review my long-range performance objectives at least once a week.	

You will now have some idea of the areas of your life where you can make improvements. If you create, prioritize and review a daily task list then you know that you are on the right track. Here are some pointers for you to follow:

- **Know yourself** – be clear about how you see the balance between work and home life. Accept your limitations but work to improve those areas that you can do something about. For example, if deadlines stress you out, make sure that you complete work well in advance. Conversely, if you work better under pressure, set tight deadlines.

  Recognize times when you work at your best – if you work best first thing in the morning, plan to do your most difficult tasks during those times. Additionally, if you are having a particularly good day, tackle tasks that you have been putting off.

  Be aware if you have a weekly pattern, for instance, do you find it difficult to get into the swing of things on Mondays but you are fine by Friday?

  Consider whether you have a monthly or yearly pattern – are there times of the year when you work better than others? How do you function when you've worked solidly for a month, including weekends?

  Learn to use your best time to think or plan, depending on which you find most difficult. You will produce more realistic plans if you are on top of your game.

  Accept that there are some things that are outside of your control. Know what you can and can't control.

  Build in time each day to do something for yourself.

- **Dealing with other people** – communicate with clients and colleagues so that everyone understands what you are trying to achieve and what your priorities are. Have respect for your time and for the time of others. Try to be proactive rather than waiting for things to come to you.

  Discuss 'distractions' with colleagues in a positive way and without blame. Let others know how you intend to deal with distractions. Learn to recognize interruptions that can help you to achieve your objectives and those which are time wasters.

- **Goals, priorities and planning** – know your goals, and objectives and prioritize! Make sure you understand how you are going to achieve your objectives, keep your focus on meeting them.

  Don't fall into the trap of dealing with urgent tasks and putting the most important tasks as a lower priority.

  Acknowledge that spending long hours in the office does not necessarily equate to being productive or producing high quality work.

  Recognize the importance of planning.

- **Your working day** – make a record of how you spend your time. Analyse your time and make sure that you are spending it achieving your objectives. Allocate sufficient time to complete tasks otherwise you may become demotivated.

  Take control. Be disciplined about how you spend your time and don't let others take control of your time.

  Work through each task to completion. Don't jump from one task to another.

- **Take action** – tackle tasks in order of importance. Don't put off difficult tasks – they won't go away. Difficult tasks will seem less daunting once you have begun to tackle them.

  Recognize that it is sometimes okay to put off doing a task for a while. Just because you are away from a task doesn't mean that you have forgotten about it. Try thinking things through while going for a walk or going to the gym. You may find that you come back to the problem refreshed and raring to go. If you are lacking energy or concentration it may be better to come back to a task when your energy levels are higher.

  Systems – take time to look at the systems you use. Ask yourself what they are used for, whether they are necessary and do they work. Work to improve your systems so that you can produce work of a higher quality in less time.

  Ask yourself whether you need to produce paperwork. If so, who needs a copy and how should you file it? Try to keep paperwork to a minimum.

Manage your working area

How tidy is your work area? Think about your work area in terms of both your physical office and where you store files on your computer. You will waste a lot of time if your desk is untidy and you cannot find papers, stationery, files, etc. Similarly, if you use a computer, take a look at your filing system. Spend some time organizing your work into appropriately named and structured files and folders. There's nothing more time wasting than trying to remember the name of a document or where you filed it.

If you are sharing a PC with your family, it may also be worthwhile setting up a second area on your hard disk (known as a 'partition') so that work and home files can be kept separate. For instance, you could use drive C:\ for personal files and drive D:\ for work files.

Self check

Look around your office, and answer the following questions?

- Have you thought about where tools and equipment such as scanners, telephones and files are best placed around the room? ❏

- Are the supplies you frequently use always to hand? ❏

- Can you always find your files and job information when you want them? ❏

- Is your work area cluttered? ❏

- Do you waste time looking for things? ❏

- Do you use all of the items that you currently have in your work area? ❏

Managing paperwork

Work out a suitable system for managing your paperwork. For example:

- **Action** – where paperwork needs to be dealt with urgently, act on it straight away. If you can't deal with it immediately, make a note of what action needs to be taken (a post-it note on the work would be good) and place it in a 'pending tray' with a due date clearly marked.

- **Read information** – read information and file if necessary. If you don't need to read it immediately but would find it useful in the future, file it in a 'reading file' and have a system for reviewing the contents of the file from time to time. Alternatively, the information may need to be passed on to another person. If so, send it complete with your comments and initials so that the person knows that you have read the information. If it is not necessary to keep the information, bin it.
- **Pending file** – have a system for reviewing the contents of this file regularly and actioning each item.

Making the telephone work for you

Many people dread making telephone calls and, if you are one of them, you may find yourself putting off making the call indefinitely. You can help yourself by making a list of people that you need to call at the start of each day, and making an effort to deal with all the calls in one go.

Self check

Do you make effective use of the telephone? Do you:

- set aside a time each day to make and receive calls? ❏
- plan each call that you make? ❏
- make a brief note of what you want to say or find out so that you are clear about the purpose of your call? ❏
- make sure you are clear, succinct and warm with the person at the other end of the phone and aim to cover what you have to say in 3 minutes? ❏

Exercise

Make yourself an action sheet like the one below. This can also be used as a record of your activities:

- for your line manager
- for yourself – you can check at the start of each day if there are tasks outstanding from the previous day
- to ensure a smooth handover to colleagues before you go on leave
- to track progress with clients and suppliers.

Monday 10 October				
List of calls	What to say	Outcome and action	To do	Status
Tim Hutton	Thank for enquiry. Paperwork will be sent out by end of play tomorrow. Is that okay?	Fine. Would also like information on product X.	Send information on product X at same time as other paperwork.	To do
Sally Gilby	Need help with ideas for marketing product X. Is she able to meet?	Yes, can help. Need to arrange a meeting.	Check diary and call Sally back after 4 pm today with meeting date.	Call back after 4 pm today.
John Bradly	Sent him blurb on product X 2 weeks ago. Has he had chance to look at it? Is he interested in puchasing it?	Is interested but wants to see demo.	Arrange for Karl to give him a call and go out to do demo. Needs to be soon as he's away on holiday from end of week.	All arranged.

You will feel much better once you have made your calls for the day. Things are often not as bad as they seem at first.

Decision making

Decision making and problem solving are things that most of us find difficult. If you find yourself procrastinating instead of taking action, have a go at using the KOALA model to help you reach your desired goals more efficiently:

Knowledge	Gather enough facts to enable you to decide how much time to allocate to a task.
Objective	Make sure you know what you are trying to achieve. If you're not sure, you will waste time skirting around the issues.
Alternatives	Think laterally. Are you approaching the problem in the most logical way or are there alternatives which might provide a better solution?
Look ahead	Do you have a vision of how your decisions will work in practice?
Action	Put your decisions into action!

Working under pressure

Stress can have a positive and negative effect on our lives – the point at which the scales tip in the wrong direction will be different for each of us. Some people work best when they have strict deadlines to adhere to; many others prefer to tackle things at a steadier pace. The secret to keeping on top of your workload is to know yourself and to understand when things are becoming too much for you. It is also a good idea to have a plan for coping if you find that the pressure is mounting out of control. Here are some ways that you can reduce the build-up of pressure:

- **Take a step back** and look at your priorities – you may find that some things just don't need to be done right away.
- **Be realistic** – are you setting yourself achievable deadlines? If you can't change current deadlines, learn not to be unrealistic for the future.
- **Communicate** – talk to people positively and constructively about how you feel rather than bottling your feelings up.
- **Take action** – don't let resentment and frustration build up. You will always feel better if you take action rather than burying your head in the sand.
- **Don't worry** – about things that you cannot change. Concentrate on those that you can.
- **Deal with the 'here and now'** – don't dwell on past experiences or things that may or may not occur in the future.

Working with your manager

It may be that your weekly tasks are set by your line manager and not by yourself. If this is the case, it is particularly important that you have a process in place to regularly feed back your progress to your manager. It is vitally important to remember the following:

- Let your manager know when you are struggling to complete tasks in the allotted time. This is not a sign of failure – progress against each task should be discussed on a regular basis as your manager will not necessarily be aware of what you are doing to meet your targets. Keeping a diary of your daily activities will help to strengthen your position.

- Your manager has a vested interest in making sure that you are able to do your job well because it will reflect badly on him or her if you don't.

- You have a right to be managed in a way that will enable you to perform to the best of your ability.

- Take a positive approach – always show yourself as someone willing to take initiative.

Summary

If you have been used to working from a traditional office and having your time managed by a line manager you may find that it comes as something of a shock to have to manage your own time. This chapter has shown that time is a resource that needs to be managed, and that working smartly will help you to enjoy both your work and leisure time. You need to plan activities in line with short-, medium- and long-term goals, and review your progress regularly against your planned objectives. Developing your time management skills will be one of the most important investments you can make.

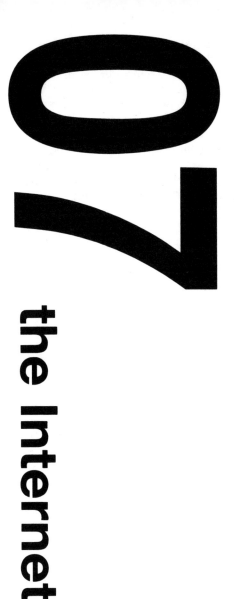

07

the Internet

In this chapter you will learn:

- about flexible working and the Internet
- how to connect to the Internet
- about Internet security

This chapter looks at the Internet and other technological innovations that have made flexible working possible. There is no doubt that access to the Internet has had a significant impact on our ability to work flexibly, but even in today's hi-tech society it is difficult to gauge just how familiar people are with the Internet and what it can do for them. Here we concentrate on ways of connecting to the Internet and on some of the security issues that may affect your ability to work flexibly.

Flexible working and the Internet

Simply put, the Internet is an international network of computers. It contains billions of pages of information and enables you to communicate almost instantaneously with people across the world.

The Internet symbolizes different things to different people. To some it will be a giant library full of interesting articles. To others it will be a set of vibrant graphical pages that bring up-to-the-minute news, weather and stock market reports. To others still it will deliver a video channel through which they can talk in real time face to face with colleagues in another location and send or receive files cheaply and efficiently.

As a flexible worker here are some of things that you can look forward to:

- tools that give you the flexibility to chat anywhere anytime
- the ability to send correspondence quickly and easily via email
- one-to-one conversations using messaging programs
- group discussions using video conferencing software
- searching for information from the comfort of your own home
- creating web pages to promote your business.

If you are not already hooked to the Internet, give it a go. It will soon become a part of your working life that you just can't do without. In fact, it's difficult to imagine how working from home was ever an option before the Internet came along.

To access the Internet (go online) you will typically need:

- a computer
- a telephone line
- a modem

- a software program that allows you to connect to the Internet
- an account with an Internet Service Provider (ISP).

Hooking up to the Internet

Billions of computers around the world are joined to the Internet via a system of cables, telephone lines, satellite and wireless radio links. Most people don't need to go to extraordinary lengths to connect to the Internet. A connection can be achieved via an ordinary telephone line and a dial-up modem attached to a PC (personal computer). However, depending on the nature of your work, you may want to take advantage of the attractive speeds and flexibility offered by the latest broadband technologies, and for this you will need a different kind of connection to the Internet. Some of the major options available to you are covered below.

Dial up-modem

Probably the cheapest and easiest way to connect to the Internet and the method used by around 80% of households in the UK (BBC website report, 10 July 2003) is via a standard telephone line and modem. The modem will convert digital information produced by your computer into electrical voltages (analogue signals) that can be sent down the telephone line. A modem at the other end will convert the analogue signals back into digital format so that the receiving computer can read them.

The advantage of this type of connection is that most people have a telephone line already installed at home and most computers these days are supplied with built-in modems. Even if you have an older machine, modems are relatively cheap to buy. If you do need to buy a modem, choose one that transmits information at 56 Kilobits per second and conforms to the V.90 standard.

The main disadvantages of connecting to the Internet in this way are speed and reliability. At a speed of 56 Kilobits per second or less, large files can take a long time to send or receive (download). Modem dial-up connections are also occasionally unreliable. Downloading large and complex files can put an extra strain on resources and result in temporary loss of access to the Internet. While these may seem like minor issues to the casual home PC user, they can quickly become major sources of frustration for the dedicated flexible worker who relies heavily on productivity and working independently. This will be particularly true if you regularly work with memory-intensive files like photo's or graphics. A dial-up modem may well have you tearing your hair out!

Moreover, speed and reliability are not the only considerations. While your modem is sending information, you will not be able to receive incoming calls on the same telephone line. If this is likely to be an issue, you should consider installing an additional telephone line dedicated solely to Internet access or, where possible, opt for a more flexible connection to the Internet such as that found through broadband.

Broadband

According to a report published by the Office of National Statistics in December 2003, 48% of UK households are now online (11.9 million) and around 17% of these use broadband. So what is broadband and why might this provide a better option than a dial-up modem for you as a flexible worker?

Digital Subscriber Line (DSL) broadband technologies allow high-speed digital data to be sent down a standard telephone line. This has several implications. Firstly, information can be transmitted at a much greater speed than via a dial-up modem. And secondly, as the technology makes use of spare capacity on your telephone line, it also means that you can use the telephone at the same time as being on the Internet. Although you will still have to pay a separate charge for your telephone line and voice calls, DSL broadband providers typically charge you a set fee per month which will give you unlimited access to the Internet.

For many flexible workers transmission speed is the main issue. With broadband you can typically expect to achieve speeds somewhere in the region of three to ten times greater than those achieved with a modem (and often more), and this is likely to have a significant impact on the quality of information that you receive. Music, video, animation and pictures will all potentially be of much higher quality if transmitted using broadband rather than a modem. And if you are considering taking part in online video conferencing sessions or even sending pictures and messages via an instant messaging program, it will be worth your while investing in broadband.

As with most things though, there are drawbacks, and with broadband the major obstacle to date has been location. You may find that unless you live in a city and in the vicinity of an exchange with broadband links, broadband is not available.

If you want to check whether broadband is available in your area of the UK, you can visit a one-stop shop such as www.broadbandchecker.co.uk that will give you availability as well as a comparison of service providers and prices. All you have to do is enter your UK postcode and telephone number (optional) and you will be given a list of services available in your area.

Due to the disparity in levels of broadband services across the UK, a number of companies have come up with alternative ways of linking into the net. According to the BBC report mentioned earlier, Scottish Hydro-Electric are helping people in remote areas of Scotland to tap into the Internet using the National Grid. Customers link into the Internet via a connector that plugs into an electricity socket in the home and are often able to send information at far greater speeds than those normally accessible through standard DSL broadband packages.

Satellite

Some Internet users in rural areas get their services via satellite links. You can choose to opt for a one-way or two-way service. A one-way service will allow you to receive information through a satellite receiver at much faster download speeds than using a dial-up modem but you will still need to use a dial-up modem to send emails and other information out to the Internet. To take advantage of this service you will need to purchase a small satellite dish and receiver and then pay a monthly fee.

As you can appreciate, operating a satellite service can be expensive and one of the ways in which the providers will keep their costs down is to limit how much traffic flows through the system. As a result you may have a limit imposed on the amount of information that you can download over a period of time. Surpassing your limit may lead to a reduction in transmission speeds. Some broadband satellite customers have found that download speeds can be reduced to levels equivalent to those of a dial-up modem.

Alternatively, you can choose to invest larger sums of money in a two-way satellite service, which will allow you to both send and receive information via the broadband satellite connection.

Whichever option you go for you may find that it is not without its problems. As anyone knows who has satellite TV, transmission can be affected by the weather. It also takes longer for information to travel via satellite because of the sheer distances involved. If you are going for satellite because you live in a rural area it may be worth checking how long it will be before you can expect technical help if you have problems.

All in all, satellite is fine for surfing the Internet, sending emails and files and accessing secure sites, but it is not yet suitable for use with Virtual Private Networks (see page 176), peer-to-peer networks (see page 207) or video conferencing.

Dial up or broadband?

The answer depends to some extent on the following:

• the nature of the work that you do
• your budget
• the availability of broadband in your area.

Before you decide, let us leave you with a summary of a study supported by the AT&T and the International Telework Association and Council.

Case study: AT&T and the International Telework Association and Council

A study by AT&T and the International Telework Association and Council in April 2003 found that there were significant differences in the operations carried out by flexible workers who use broadband as opposed to those who use a dial-up modem. The sample for the online survey was drawn from a panel of approximately 900,000 households, felt to be representative of the online US population. Of those surveyed, 71% with broadband used the Internet to find information as opposed to 54% with a dial-up connection; 36% sent large files as opposed to only 14% with dial up; 16% took part in telephone conferences as compared with only 10% of those with dial-up access and a greater percentage of broadband users engaged in group work such as jointly managing work and files. The study concluded that having high-speed Internet access through broadband enables flexible workers to work more flexibly and productively and is hugely beneficial. For more details of this study, visit the International Telework Association and Council website at www.workingfromanywhere.org.

Whatever the state of play regarding broadband in your area it seems clear that the provision of broadband services is set to increase. In addition, newer, faster and cheaper technologies are being introduced which should hopefully iron out the disparity between rural communities and cities, between flexible users and businesses.

Internet security

Although the Internet has brought phenomenal benefits in terms of mass communication, access to information and marketing opportunities, it is not without its challenges. One of the biggest headaches for both individuals and companies alike is the issue of security. Once a system is connected to the outside world via the Internet it becomes vulnerable to attack from viruses and unscrupulous hackers. While it is relatively easy to protect an individual laptop or PC from prying eyes, it is much more difficult to safeguard systems that are sharing resources over the Internet.

As a flexible worker you are increasingly likely to rely on technology to keep in regular contact with your employees or clients and you may not appreciate your PC until the day that something goes wrong. If your PC goes down you can find yourself cut off from the outside world and unable to function for substantial periods of time.

What can you do to protect yourself?

There are several ways in which you can shield your machine from attack. As a minimum precaution you should install a firewall and anti-virus software. If you are accessing company resources remotely it is likely that additional security measures such as passwords and data encryption will also be in place. The nature of the beast is such that no matter how strong the barricades, there will always be hackers who have a vested interest in developing new ways for breaking through. It will pay to keep your lines of defence strong. It is possible for hackers to access your machine remotely and:

- view files
- run programs that collect email addresses from your address book and use them for marketing purposes
- use viruses to disable or destroy your system.

To hackers, breaking through organizations' defences can be even more alluring. Apart from being motivated by malicious intent, many hackers find accessing credit card details, health details or politically sensitive information, a very lucrative business.

Firewalls

A physical firewall is a structure that is erected to prevent fire from spreading from one area to another and destroying everything in its path. The concept of an IT firewall is based on a similar premise. It is a piece of hardware or software that protects a private system or network from potentially harmful material coming in from the outside world via the Internet.

Firewalls can prevent an outsider from logging on to a machine on a private network. They work by screening each packet of information coming in from or going out to the Internet, and filtering out those that are undesirable.

You can configure a firewall by creating a set of filters that determine which packets of information should be allowed through and which should be rejected. Among other things, a firewall can be set to:

- Reject information that contains undesirable text.
- Prevent traffic from suspicious IP (Internet Protocol) addresses permeating your system (every PC on the Internet is identifiable by a unique number known as an IP address and the firewall can be set to reject information from specific addresses).
- Recognize domain names that provide acceptable material and conversely, those that are considered unsuitable.

The aim is to get a balance between allowing the right kind of traffic in from the Internet (after all, the main purpose of using the Internet in the first place is to have access to a wide range of information), while blocking traffic that is harmful or destructive.

As an individual user you might be as well to start off accepting the firewall defaults set by the computer's operating program. You can then adjust the settings if you find that you are getting nuisance traffic. A large company will usually employ a network administrator to set the filters. The job of the administrator will be to control Internet traffic so that only business critical information is allowed through and potentially harmful traffic rejected. For example, an administrator might set filters to allow all incoming emails but restrict user access to specified websites only.

Viruses

Like its biological equivalent, a computer virus is a software program that can severely disable your system or even render it unusable. A virus will generally attach itself to a program (such as a word processor or spreadsheet program) and make a copy of itself. The virus will then sit in the computer's memory and scan for other susceptible programs to infect. Each time an infected program runs, the virus will run too and so the process goes on. In this way viruses spread quickly from one system to another. Viruses are usually triggered by some event or action such as a date or time.

Over the years, developers of virus programs have become increasingly more devious, finding ways to make sure that viruses sit in memory and stay active for the entire time that a machine is running. However, with recent developments in technology, the opportunities for virus invasion have been somewhat reduced and the threat is less pervasive than it was, say, 20 years ago.

Viruses are transmitted through:

- downloading infected files from the Internet
- opening an infected email attachment
- transferring data on to your PC from an infected source (memory stick, floppy disk, CD ROM).

Some viruses are relatively harmless, others however are much more destructive, to the point where they will re-format your hard disk and destroy your data.

There are different types of infections:

- **Worms** – a worm attaches itself to a weak security link in a network and can make a copy of itself to then pass on to the next susceptible server.
- **Trojan horses** – a Trojan horse is a computer program that is disguised as something else. For instance, it may masquerade as a game that you can download off the Internet but in fact when you open it its purpose is to destroy your data.
- **Email viruses** – email is thought to be the most widely used Internet application and it is estimated that by 2005, 35 billion emails will sent daily. As such, email is an ideal medium for spreading viruses or for using devious means to collect and make use of addresses in personal address books.

In the late 1990s, the infamous Melissa virus wreaked havoc upon thousands of unsuspecting email users. The virus was embedded in a Microsoft Word email attachment and as soon as a recipient opened the attachment the virus was sent to 50 people in their address book. Not surprisingly, the virus spread like wild fire.

Although anti-virus software is a must, there is a degree of protection that is down to you. It will pay you to be vigilant and follow a few simple rules:

- As new viruses hit the market, anti-virus software suppliers release upgrades to eliminate them. It is important to make sure that you download new upgrades when prompted.
- It is equally important to make sure that you install anti-virus software and firewalls on all equipment, including the laptop that you take out on the road.
- Make sure you regularly take a back-up copy of all-important data.
- Only download Internet files that come from a reputable source.
- Only open emails that come from a recognized source.
- Be wary of emails that contain attachments. If you doubt the source, don't open the attachment.
- If an email attachment has a .doc (Word), .xls (Excel), .gif or .jpg (images) extension, they are likely to be harmless. Attachments with an .exe, .com or .vbs extension are programs that will run once you open them and may result in extensive damage if they contain viruses. Don't open them.
- If you are using a Microsoft product, make sure that macro virus protection is set as an option on the Tools menu and don't run macros unless you know what they do. Viruses hidden in macro programs often go undetected by traditional virus software.

Passwords, encryption and authentication

Companies have historically been reluctant to allow remote workers access to company files while away from the traditional place of work. The main reason for this has been a general lack of confidence in the technology designed to protect private systems from invasion. However, due to technological enhancements, this has changed somewhat. Companies have growing confidence in the password, encryption and authentication systems that can be used to provide a shield from the outside world. If you are a flexible worker it is likely that, at some stage in your working life, you will end up completing these security checks if you need to log on to a private network remotely.

Passwords

A password is simply a private code you use to identify yourself in order to gain entry to a particular website. Unfortunately, passwords are one of the easiest codes for hackers to break. They can be picked up electronically or even deduced from other personal data that you enter. They can also be picked up by word of mouth. To protect your password files:

- where possible, change your password frequently
- never tell anyone else your password
- never write your password down
- use different passwords for each public website
- use different passwords for personal and company systems.

Encryption

Many organizations such as online banks or retail outfits use encryption as a method of transferring information securely across the Internet. In simple terms encryption means that information you enter online will be scrambled in such a way that although possibly visible to the outside world, it will be unreadable. The system at the other end will then unscramble the message using private codes. In practice, the process is often much more complex than this with a combination of sophisticated coding systems used as the basis for data encryption.

Authentication systems

Authentication systems are systems that check for highly personal and unique data with which to identify you. Popular authentication systems include:

- voice
- face
- iris recognition
- fingerprint scanners
- smartcards (store unique identification profiles).

These types of system have come on in leaps and bounds. However, it will probably be some time before they are in general circulation. Each system has its pluses and minuses. Voice, face and fingerprint identification systems provide assurance that the data collected is unique for each individual, but some are costly and difficult to transport around. Smartcards are potentially open to misuse as they are more likely to be stolen or used by more than one person. It may also be prohibitively costly to install smartcard readers for all employees working off site.

However, although no one authentication system is perfect and it may be some time before organizations feel confident enough to allow remote workers to tap into private data networks, the time will come when there will be sufficient confidence in encryption and authentication technology to boost the confidence of the e-commerce community.

Case study: Ben

Ben is a National Health System manager. He works from a regional office 4 days a week and from home one day a week. On the day that Ben works from home he would like to be able to link into the company network and access his work files but he recognizes that there are important security issues that need to be ironed out before this becomes a reality.

'My department adheres to a strict patient confidentiality charter and consequently, needs to be certain that remote data access is secure. At present the organization is investigating a range of security tools including the use of smartcards.

'Although this is a fantastic step in the right direction for me because it means that I will be able to work at home more often, I can see that there may be some problems with the trialling of the smartcards. For example, as systems are shared it may be all too tempting for one person to log on with their smartcard and then allow a colleague to access the same system without going through a formal log in process.

'Having said that, I know that enhancements to smartcard technology are currently being trialled. These include tracking who uses the card, when, for how long and what type of data has been accessed. This should highlight some areas of misuse as people should only have access to data that is related to their role. It will soon become obvious if the person logged on to the system has been accessing files outside of their authority.'

Digital signatures

Authentication systems, such as digital signatures, are used to reassure you that a message has been sent from a bona fides source and has not been tampered with along the way. A digital signature is the electronic equivalent of a traditional paper signature that is unique to the sender and is used as a stamp of authentication.

In order to create a digital signature, information has to go through rigorous assessment using both encryption and authentication techniques. If a digital signature is approved you will be notified that the data you are receiving has a signature attached.

Protecting yourself from fraud
You should never give out private or confidential information unless you can be absolutely sure that a site is secure. Most website addresses begin with http:// but a secure site will start with https:// (the additional 's' in the address indicating that it is secure).

A site may contain a mixture of secure and insecure pages. If a page is secure you should be able to see a closed padlock or unbroken key symbol at the bottom of the screen. You should also receive a warning if you are about to leave a secure page and move to one that is insecure. It is all too easy to click the mouse to confirm that you are happy to proceed without thinking about the implications.

Many companies who collect sensitive information operate a technology known as SSL (Secure Socket Layer) technology. This means that the information you send is encrypted or scrambled in such a way that it is unreadable by anyone else other than the organization it is intended for. It is then unscrambled upon receipt at the other end. If you want to check the level of website security, position your mouse over the padlock or key symbol. You should see a figure, which represents the encryption level. An online financial institution will usually have an encryption level of 128 and an online shop will typically have a level of 40.

To ensure your online security:

• Read a company's terms and conditions carefully.
• Make sure that in addition to electronic contact details the company has a bona fides contact name, address and telephone number.
• There should be an option for you to refuse permission for your details to be disclosed to other parties. Take it.
• Never give out credit card details in an email.
• Always check your financial statements so that any fraudulent transactions can be picked up quickly.

Virtual Private Networks

In the early days of computing many PCs operated on a stand-alone basis. This meant that an individual would create and save work on to a PC and then transfer information back and forwards via a floppy disk. As this was a time-consuming and costly exercise companies soon started to create cable and phone links between PCs (networks) so that resources and data could be shared easily and efficiently. These early networks were typically operated on a regional basis and were known as Local Area Networks (LANs).

As the opportunities for global communications and commerce grew, many organizations came to appreciate the benefits of extending private networks beyond their own geographical region. Many subscribed to expensive leased lines in an effort to create secure and dependable Wide Area Networks (WANs). However, the Internet explosion opened up new and cheaper options. Suddenly, here was the technology to do business on a global basis and for a fraction of the cost (phone calls to the Internet being charged at local rather than international rates). With connection costs reduced, the main issues became ones of reliability and security. How can you send private information stored on a company network across a public network (the Internet) and keep it safe from prying eyes?

And so came the birth of Virtual Private Networks (VPNs). VPNs provide a private connection to the Internet. No matter where a company is based, workers with access to the company VPN can dial up to the Internet for the cost of a local call and log on to the company network. Journalists working for a London based international news agency for example, may be stationed in South Africa, Indonesia or the USA but be able to tap into company resources as if they were located in London.

VPNs depend on the use of encryption, authentication and tunnelling systems to make sure that only those with permission can see the data. Encryption techniques are used to scramble the data, authentication systems are used to indentify the source and integrity of the data, and tunnelling systems are designed to make sure that the data gets routed to the right address. The user of the VPN should not be aware at any time that their data is shooting off across a public network.

Apart from the issue of security, speed and connectivity are also important considerations. Performance can be reduced by the amount of bandwidth taken up with security and routing data as well as the transmission of company data. For this reason, some ISPs are reluctant to allow users to access VPNs unless they use a dial-up connection. However, while there are still some issues surrounding VPNs they are likely to become an increasingly popular option for companies with flexible workers.

Case study: Access Migration

Access Migration is one of the UK's leading migration consultancies, providing a range of services for potential migrants to Australia, New Zealand and Canada. Director, Kerry Martin, runs the day-to-day business from offices in Wellingborough. Senior Migration Consultant for the company, Michael Fidler, works out of an office in Brisbane, Australia.

Having a global business model is fundamental to the success of Access Migration. Kerry and the UK team are available to meet with clients face to face, and Michael is ideally placed to deal with the relevant authorities on a local level in Australia or New Zealand. When Kerry's team leave the UK office for the day, Michael continues to work on client visa applications, often having issues resolved by the time the UK office opens for business the next morning.

Initially, Michael and Kerry used video conferencing software and email to keep each other abreast of progress. However, in recent months they have also invested in a contact management system, operating through a VPN over the Internet.

Using a VPN has brought numerous business benefits. Client information is now held in a central database and can be easily accessed from either location. Data is synchronized at regular intervals throughout the day so when Michael opens a file he can always be sure that he is working on the most up-to-date version of the file. And the risk of compromising client confidentiality is minimized because only Access Migration consultants with a secure user ID and password can tap into the network.

Michael says that 'initially we had some problems with setting up the system but now that these have been ironed out having a VPN has totally revolutionized the way we work.'

Summary

Security is one of the biggest challenges facing the Internet industry, but there is a range of tools available to help you to combat security threats: anti-virus software, firewalls, email scanning software, passwords and encryption.

Due to the popularity of email, email is one of the easiest targets for hackers wanting to invade your system as it can be used to transmit viruses and/or collect a list of addresses from your address book. It is important to keep one step ahead of hackers and keep your security systems up to date.

Virtual Private Networks (VPNs) are increasingly used as a means of providing secure access to private company data over the Internet.

08

communication tools

In this chapter you will learn:

- about instant messaging
- about video conferencing
- about audio conferencing
- about email
- about telephone tools and services
- about Internet telephony and mobile phones

This chapter will concentrate on the practicalities of communicating with the outside world via telephone, email and the Internet. If you have access to the Internet you have some really exciting tools at your fingertips including Internet phones and programs that let you talk in real time, face to face with other computer users who can be anywhere else in the world. You no longer have to pick up the phone or be in the same room as colleagues or clients to start up a conversation, and you don't need to schedule meetings months in advance because you work in a remote location. You can 'meet up' as often as you like, providing that you have the same software installed on your machines and are free at the same time. There are two types of program that are excellent for communicating at a distance: Instant Messaging and Video Conferencing software.

Instant Messaging

An Instant Messaging program is exactly as its name suggests. It is a program that allows two people to send real-time messages to each other on screen. One person sends a message, the other replies, the first person responds and so on. Brilliant if you want to have a one-to-one or private chat with a work colleague or your manager.

Available programs include AOL Messenger, MSN Messenger, Yahoo! Messenger and ICQ. They are all easy to use and free to download from the individual company website. The programs are all similar in look and feel and which one you decide to use is really just a matter of personal preference.

How do I get started?

It is really easy to get started. All you need to do is add a buddy or friend into a contact list on the program. When your contact is online you begin a conversation. If you are using Yahoo! Messenger, for instance, you can set the preferences so that you get a knocking sound on the screen when your contact is online and a yellow smiley face will be displayed next to their name.

To open the messaging window all you have to do is double-click on their name. From there you type your message and click the 'Send' button. Your contact will see the message on their screen almost straight away and can send their reply back to you. These programs can be incredibly useful if you want to throw a quick idea by a colleague or ask a question of one of your online colleagues.

Using a web camera

If you and your contact each have a web camera, you can use messaging programs as well as video conferencing software to broadcast live video pictures at the same time as chatting.

Once you have installed the webcam software (which is usually relatively straightforward), you start the webcam and invite someone on your contact list to view it. When the webcam begins broadcasting you will see the image that is being broadcast on your screen. If your camera has a built-in microphone or you have an independent microphone attached to your PC (personal computer) you should also be able to hear the other person talking. Alternatively, go for a wireless experience with a bluetooth-enabled headset (see Chapter 9, Flexible working on the move).

This is one of those times when it will pay to have a broadband connection. With a dial-up modem you are more likely to get a broken, jerky picture due to the slower transmission speeds. With a picture delivered via broadband the image is going to be much slicker and smoother.

Video conferencing

Where Instant Messaging programs are designed for one on one, video conferencing software is useful when a group of people want to get together as a group and chat over the Internet.

For video conferencing you and your colleagues will each need:

- a computer connected to the Internet (preferably via broadband)
- video conferencing software like Microsoft NetMeeting
- a web camera
- microphone
- speakers.

If you are a Windows 2000 user Microsoft NetMeeting will already by installed on your machine. To use it, click the 'Start' button followed by 'Programs', 'Accessories', 'Communications' and then 'NetMeeting'. NetMeeting is an excellent piece of software for:

- chatting face to face via a video link
- sharing ideas
- taking a snapshot with your video camera and displaying the image on a whiteboard for discussion
- sharing computer programs and files
- sending pictures and graphics
- recording meeting notes and action items through its text-based chat program.

Case study: Video conferening

The benefits of video conferencing are well reported. A BBC news report on 25 March 2004 told of how Michael Foale the astronaut talked to school children in Sheffield via a video conference link direct from the International Space Station.

A BBC news report on 25 February 2004 reported how miners in the former Soviet Republic of Kyrgyz learn from their industrial counterparts in Africa, Europe and North America via a video link.

The case study scenarios may not be quite what you had in mind for your venture into video conferencing, but the point is that there are limitless reasons for getting together in a virtual environment. You can hold a meeting with international clients, you can embark on a distance-learning course to enhance your skills, and you can demonstrate your products online.

Audio conferencing

As well as video conferencing, you can also take part in audio conferences. This is where a group of people can converse on the phone at the same time. It is similar to video conferencing but without the picture.

Case study: Rob

Rob works for the National Health Service. He manages a team of people who all function as flexible workers.

'Sometimes it is difficult to get everyone together in the same place at the same time. More often than not, we end up setting a date and time for a conference call, as it's the only way we can get together in the week. Each member of the team has access to a special audio phone that looks like a huge spider. We can all hear each other clearly and we can join in the conversation as needed. We usually elect a chairperson to control the flow of the conversation. The chair decides who speaks, when and for how long, just like a chair in a face-to-face meeting.

'There are some downsides to it though. For one, without a chairperson you need to have good meeting skills, otherwise you end up chipping in when someone else is speaking. Also, it is sometimes difficult to tell who is speaking because people sound very similar. And you don't get quite the same rapport that you get from sitting in the same room with these people!'

Email

Email (electronic mail) is by far the most popular type of program used on the Internet today. It is used primarily for sending messages, photos and other material that would otherwise be sent by traditional post. Most people are familiar with email, but if you are going to work flexibly it will become one of your biggest assets. Here is a quick summary:

- Emails can reach the other side of the world in a matter of minutes as opposed to the days that it may take by traditional mail – and all for the cost of a local phone call rather than hefty international post charges!
- Email makes it easy to stay in contact by sending short, informal and spontaneous messages. It also means that you are likely to receive quicker responses to letters or enquiries, which can save you substantial business time.
- Most email programs allow you to send attachments. You can include photo, picture, video and sound files.
- Companies can keep you up to date with their latest offerings if you sign up to receive e-newsletters.
- And, most importantly, you need never be out of touch. You can send and receive emails while you are on the move.

Providing you have the equipment to log on to the Internet, and a web-based Internet account, there are lots of places to connect: airports, train stations, Internet cafés, telephone kiosks, restaurants, service stations and the local library.

Online stamps

Busy flexible workers take note. Instead of buying stamps over the counter you can purchase Smart Stamps from Royal Mail online:

- choose from a range of mailing options
- buy national and international stamps and print them directly on to labels or envelopes via an ordinary printer
- deposit the mail in an ordinary post box.

You can pay for the service on a monthly basis or subscribe for an annual fee. For the fee you will receive the software, which can then be downloaded onto your PC. Any monies spent on stamps will be deducted from a pre-paid account, which you can top up using a credit or debit card. For further details visit: www.royalmail.com/smartstamp

Managing email

Although email can replace the more cumbersome and costly 'snail mail' it still presents some challenges:

- You might find that you cannot access your usual email program on the move. If this is the case, consider setting up a free web-based email account through Hotmail, Yahoo! or Lycos.
- As a flexible worker you are likely to rely on email as your link to the outside world. Don't fall into the trap of constantly checking your inbox for new mail, and refrain from answering non-urgent emails instead of getting on with more important work. This downtime can have an adverse effect on your productivity.
- Stick to a regular time to check emails each day (e.g. first thing in the morning and at lunchtime). Shut down your email application in between times.
- Be consistent in the way you approach emails; open each email and do one of four things: reply, save, forward or delete. Ideally your inbox should be empty at the end of each day.

- Save emails into aptly named folders such as 'To do'.
- Ask colleagues not to copy you in on other people's mail unless absolutely necessary.
- Keep a copy of Sent messages that are important, but make sure that you delete Sent items frequently.

Spam

If you work from home there will be lots of distractions to prevent you from getting on with the job in hand. One of the most frustrating and time-wasting aspects of email is spam. Spam is the electronic equivalent of the junk mail that drops through your letter box. As soon as you start using the Internet, you will notice an increase in the amount of junk mail that you receive. There are companies whose sole purpose it is to scan the Internet looking for email addresses or information that they can sell on to other companies. Just be aware that every time you enter a website or give out information across the net there are companies that have a vested interest in harvesting that information so that they or others can make use of it.

Spim

Spim is the term now being used to represent unwanted mail (spam) delivered via Instant Messaging (IM). In an effort to reduce spim, IBM have developed software that checks incoming messages for a code allocated by the user to friends and family. If the code is received the message will be allowed through. If it isn't, this, and further messages from the same sender will be deleted.

To try and minimize spam and spim:

- Don't open junk mail.
- Don't follow instructions to remove yourself from mailing lists. By replying you are confirming the validity of your email address.
- Don't give out your email address unless you are sure of the person/company to whom you are giving it.
- Don't load a website address that is advertised via junk mail. By clicking on a website link you may get a cookie (a packet of data) stored on your machine that contains personal information about your buying habits, etc.

If you are receiving abnormal amounts of junk mail there are several things that you can do to help yourself:

- Check your Internet Service Provider's (ISP's) policy on how to deal with junk mail.
- Visit the Advertising Standards Authority website at www.asa.org.uk for advice and information.
- Install free anti-spamming software such as MailWasher available from www.mailwasher.net.
- Set options in your email program to filter out unwanted email. You can filter out emails that contain specific text or that come from particular addresses.

TIP: If you are using a Yahoo! or similar web-based email account you can turn SpamGuard on and off. If SpamGuard is on, Yahoo! will deliver all suspect mail to a 'Bulk' folder and delete it 1 month later if it hasn't been opened. You can help Yahoo! to identify spam by clicking the 'Spam' button when spam mail comes into your mail box. Conversely you can choose the 'Not spam' button when bulk mail is not spam.

Style and content

In addition to the threat of viruses and junk mail, there are other concerns over the sending of email. Unlike a traditional letter where you might spend several hours mulling over the style and thinking about what you want to say, email is a much more informal and spontaneous method of communication and, as such, is likely to be more easily misinterpreted. You are much more likely to knock out an email and hit the send button without thinking about whether the style and content are appropriate for your audience, than you would when sending a hand-written letter. Once you hit the send button there is nothing that you can do to retrieve the message so it is a good idea to get into the habit of reading through each email before you send.

TIP: Rather than composing a new message each time you want to reply to an email, the easiest way of replying is to hit the 'Reply' button. This will put the sender's name in the address box and all you have to do is write the text. Occasionally you may also want to forward the message to someone else and you can do this using the 'Forward' function. However, in both cases it is very important to check the address lines of the message and make sure that it is directed to your intended recipient only.

There are endless stories of people accidentally sending mail to the wrong people or forwarding mail intended for their colleagues to their boss!

Codes of practice

Like traditional postal mail, email is routed through several servers before it reaches its final destination. Someone who has access to those servers can intercept mail at any point. It is all the more surprising to find then, that until recent years, few organizations adopted a formal code of practice in relation to email. In contrast to the regulations that exist within many organizations with regard to the sending of printed information on headed paper, the rules governing the sending of email content have been much more lax.

All sorts of information is transmitted under the auspices of company email; information that can be found incriminating or negligent in a court of law. Many companies are now wising up to this as the number of legal test cases involving email have been on the increase. In recent years email content has been used as evidence of defamation, association with inappropriate materials and internal personnel disputes. Email constitutes published material and as such it can be found libellous. As a rule of thumb you should never write anything in an email that you wouldn't write in an open letter or postcard.

TIP: To be on the safe side it is a good idea to purchase software like MAILsweeper to check incoming and outgoing email for appropriateness.

Telephone tools and services

One of the biggest worries of home workers is how to handle telephone calls when you are away from your desk. Worry not. There is a variety of tools and services available to make your life easier.

If you are an employee of a company, ask whether there is a system in place whereby someone else can field your calls. If there is, make sure that your department has as much information as possible so that phone calls can be handled efficiently on your behalf.

Answer phones and services

If you have no external support, make use of technology. You can purchase an answer phone or utilize answering services provided by telephone companies. The benefit of using technology is that you can pick and choose which messages to deal with and which to leave until later, especially if you have a system that allows you to hear the message as it's being left.

TIP: Although messaging services are available on most single standard business telephone lines, we advise that you check with your supplier to make sure that there is no conflict with other products and services that you have. For example, some alarm equipment is not compatible with messaging services.

Personal answering services

If you are running a business from home you might prefer to have the phone personally answered rather than using an answer machine. There is a number of companies who specialize in taking calls when you are away from the phone. For examples of such companies, visit the following websites: www.message-pad.com; www.moneypennyuk.com and www.verbatim-cc.co.uk.

Internet telephony

Using conventional phone lines to make long-distance calls may soon be a thing of the past. Until now traditional phone companies have been able to charge premium rates for inter-state or international phone calls. However, in addition to a raft of companies that now offer cheap rate international calls over conventional lines, you can also make long-distance calls over the Internet for the price of a local call. The technology associated with sending voice data over the Internet is known as Voice over Internet Protocol (VoIP).

Although the main benefit is chiefly one of cost, there are also tremendous benefits to be had from integrating VoIP systems with company networks. Companies can route calls quickly and efficiently between international offices and make internal calls free of charge.

The beauty of VoIP is that it can work with most networks: Virtual Private Networks (VPNs), Local Area Networks (LANs) or wireless. In fact, many telecommunications companies are already using VoIP to route calls over long distances and across a range of different networks and technologies. Apart from slight variations in service that can come from bandwidth and transmission speeds, the services are very successful. Some telecomms companies and ISPs have now come round to offering deals to encourage small businesses to get on the VoIP band wagon.

Case study: Terry

Terry is a litigation specialist working for an international firm of lawyers. The firm is based in the UK but has satellite offices in Australia and New York. Terry's work involves preparing international law suits, and takes him to all three offices. The offices are linked via a VPN integrated with a VoIP system.

'It doesn't matter what office I'm working out of. As soon as I arrive I simply log on to the company network using a secure password. If I'm working in the New York office I can see my files just like I can when I'm at my desk in Croydon.

'As the VoIP system is linked into the company network, incoming telephone calls from clients are automatically routed to the phone on the desk beside me, irrespective of where the caller is calling from. The system works so smoothly that clients calling from the UK are completely unaware that I may be sitting at a desk overlooking the Brisbane River. And when I want to make outgoing calls I press a few keys and call up numbers from my electronic phone book.'

Case study: Work Global

Work Global is a fascinating work/life balance initiative. The company operates out of the Outer Hebrides – an area of Scotland where you might expect work to be hard to come by. Not so, thanks to some progressive thinking by Work Global. The Hebrides has a highly skilled and motivated labour force that enjoys the lifestyle offered by the region and, in an effort to support these people, Work Global has attracted global e-working contracts to the region. For more information visit: http://www.work-global.com/.

How do I get to use VoIP?

There are several options open to you. Depending upon your VoIP system and equipment, you can send calls:

- directly from one PC to another
- from a PC to a phone
- from a phone to a phone.

Before deciding which system to set up it is worth checking out the websites of a few telecommunications companies for other Internet Phone (IP) products.

PC to PC

Calls can be made from one PC to another completely free of charge if you have an always-on connection to the Internet. For this you will need to have a multimedia PC with microphone and speakers, a digitizing sound card and a connection to the Internet.

Many of the current operating systems contain software that allows you to make VoIP calls. For instance, Microsoft Windows 2000 includes voice transmission with Netmeeting and Microsoft Windows XP provides a similar function through Messenger.

PC to phone

There was a time when phoning someone meant picking up a handset, pressing a series of buttons and waiting to be connected. These days voice calls can be made without a physical handset. You access the service through a virtual telephone on the screen. You simply dial the number using your mouse or keypad and click to connect. The call from your PC is then routed along the Internet to the local telephone system in your destination country. Here are some of the features that you can expect:

- You can call any landline or mobile phone in the world.
- The cost per minute is the same wherever you are calling.

Callserve at www.callserve.com and Vonage at www.vongage.com provide a software phone service.

You can purchase an adaptor known as an Analogue Telephone Adaptor (ATA) to convert your analogue phone signals into digital signals that can be sent over your PC. Some telecomms companies also throw in an adaptor as part of the service.

Phone to phone

Internet phones look like normal phones but instead of connecting into the usual socket in the wall, they connect into a router.

TIP: You may have to adjust your firewall settings in order to get your computer to work with your VoIP. Ask your VoIP vendor for advice before purchasing the software.

Case study: All in a day's work

'My name is Michael Blackburn, and I work in the BT (British Telecom) Exact strategy team. I live in Paris and often work from home. But I also have a desk at BT Centre in London. Twenty years ago that just wouldn't have been possible. Back then, I'd have been very out of touch and my home fax and phone bills would have been horrific!

'Now, part of this problem is resolved by a BT broadband voice trial I'm involved in. Basically, I have a small adapter that fits between my phone and my router/ADSL modem in France. This converts my analogue voice calls to digital. They are then carried, using internet protocol (IP), down my broadband connection, over the public internet, to Birmingham. From there, they're routed over the UK PSTN network to whoever I'm calling. It works in reverse too, so I have a Birmingham number that rings through to my flat in Paris! I make all my calls with this and it costs a great deal less than making international calls.

'Like many of BT's home workers, I also use a service that allows me to choose where I want my calls delivered when I'm away from home. This means I just have to give people one number where they can contact me, whether I'm out and about using my mobile, sitting at my desk in London or by my broadband voice phone in Paris. One of the benefits is that if you call me on my mobile and I'm not available or it's engaged, your call will go through to an answering service and I have that set up to send me voice messages as email. So I get an email with a WAV file as an attachment and I can play the message back on my PC.

Secure Internet access

'On the data side, I use the broadband connection and SIA (Secure Internet Access), a service that is being piloted across BT for home working. What it means is that, when I am in Paris, I can create a Virtual Private Network over the public Internet and the result is exactly like being on the LAN (Local Area Network) in the office. I log on in the morning and can be online all day. So if the CEO is doing a webcast, for example, I can watch it from my flat in Paris with reasonable quality. It's just like being in the office really. I am also beginning to explore areas of data conferencing – for example, BT has a conferencing service called MeetMe where you can share a whiteboard or a presentation online while you are having a voice conference call and I think that could be very useful.

'Overall, I find I can work very efficiently and cost-effectively at home. And while you do need to go to some meetings – I don't think you can do without them completely – I can do an awful lot by email and phone. I rarely feel out of touch and I think I get the best of both worlds. Some things are better done face to face and going to the office gives me the variety I need. From a personal point of view, it's more than worth it. Basically, the technology allows me to live in France – my partner is French – and if I didn't work in both places, I simply wouldn't see him as much as I do.'

Case study reproduced in full with kind permission from BT. For further information on the way forward with BT visit: http://www.btplc.com/Innovation/ForwardThinking/index.htm.

All in all there are substantial savings to be had for large corporates and small businesses alike using IP telephony. For future developments keep an eye on www.voip.org.uk, a website dedicated to IP telephony in the UK.

Mobile phones

It is probably true to say that of all the communication tools that have changed the way we work, the mobile phone is pretty much top of the list. With the way in which mobile phones have developed over the last few years it is easy to forget that their primary function is to send and receive calls on the move. For many flexible workers, that's exactly what they represent – the flexibility to keep in touch from anywhere. For an increasing number of flexible workers though, the mobile phone has become a tool to access the Internet while travelling.

Mobile phone packages

Unfortunately, advances in technology have been accompanied by a bewildering array of mobile phone packages. If you sign up for a long-term contract, many operators throw in the price of a phone free of charge. If you opt for a 'pay as you go' package you may have to purchase your own phone.

Contract terms and conditions vary among providers and there are generally lots of deals to be had, so it pays to shop around. The main providers all seem to have reasonable network coverage so your main considerations will be:

- How many minutes you estimate you will use per month.
- How many text messages you anticipate sending.
- Whether you will need to access the Internet either directly on your phone or by using your phone as a modem with a laptop computer.

Using your mobile abroad

If you intend to use your mobile phone abroad you may have to register it for international use. Make sure that you check out the rates before you go. The easiest way to do this is to look for a list of roaming charges on your provider's website. Generally you will pay less per minute if you are on a contract compared to 'pay as you go'. But beware; you can run up substantial bills if you are not careful. UK companies have to pay fees to use mobile networks in other countries and they will pass these charges on to you. In addition to paying to make calls you may also have to pay to receive incoming calls.

However, it's not all doom and gloom. Providing you budget properly, international roaming services mean that you can make phone calls without the inconvenience of finding public phone boxes or carrying local currency. Most companies also save unanswered calls to an answering service and you can pick them up at any stage of your journey.

Mobile phone technology

It wasn't so long ago that mobile phones were the size of a brick and had the functionality to suit. Many phones are now the size of a credit card and have the ability to operate as a mini PC. The latest wireless devices, for example, are perfect for receiving small packets of information over the Internet, such as share prices, news headlines, sports updates and email. Some can also pick up your location and tell you where the nearest petrol station or restaurant is.

Most mobile phones currently use a Global System for Mobile technology (GSM) that connects to the Internet. However, you are likely to see an increase in the number of people using General Packet Radio Service (GPRS) and Universal Mobile Telecommunications Systems (UMTS) technologies. These third generation mobile technologies are collectively known as 3G and look set to add an extra dimension to the way we work on the move. GPRS provides a much speedier connection to the Internet and UMTS will allow you to receive video and audio. Although GPRS is expensive in comparison to a home Internet connection, it has made many things available to mobile users, which were not previously viable:

- sending multi-media messages (text, sound and pictures)
- accessing a cut-down version of the Internet
- sending and receiving emails and email attachments
- connecting your mobile phone to a laptop or handheld PC and surfing the web.

In practical terms, GPRS means that many more of us are likely to send and receive files over the Internet and carry out daily tasks like banking and shopping online using our mobile phones. You will also be able to use your mobile phone to receive music and video, take part in live video conferencing sessions and download directions to your next location when travelling.

Summary

Instant Messaging is a type of program that allows two people to send real-time messages to each other over a screen, and you can use a web camera with both messaging and video conferencing programs.

Unsolicited email is known as spam. Luckily, there are lots of things that you can do to prevent spam becoming a nuisance.

You can use mobile phones for both voice calls and Internet access, and you can make voice calls across the Internet for a fraction of the cost of traditional phone calls.

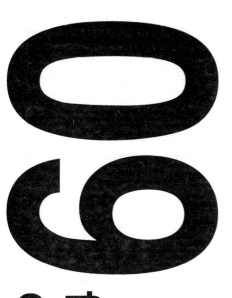

09

flexible working on the move

In this chapter you will learn:

- about working on the move
- about wireless communication
- about wireless standards
- about wireless access to the Internet at home
- about wireless on the move

Flexible working has taken on a whole new meaning with recent technological innovations making it possible to work from just about anywhere and at any time. Gone are the days of being tied to a PC (personal computer) at your desk. Now you can type up an agenda for a meeting on the train, catch up with the latest news via your mobile phone, pick up emails from an Internet café or host a worldwide discussion group from the comfort of your own home.

The increasing range of flexible working options open to us today can be attributed to two key developments: the Internet and wireless technologies. Between them, they have revolutionized the way we work on the move.

The growth of the Internet has meant that flexible workers have:

- access to a giant library of information
- the potential to share files quickly and easily with colleagues and clients working in other locations
- the option to hook up to a company network from a location other than the company office
- the ability to communicate with people around the world at the touch of a few buttons.

The second and perhaps most significant catalyst to change, wireless technologies, has provided a way for flexible workers to access the Internet on the move, without being tied to a PC with cables. Wireless access to the Internet has taken the concept of 'flexibility' to a new dimension.

The previous chapter provided an overview of the Internet and methods of connection. This chapter will concentrate on technology that is available to help you work smarter on the move.

Working on the move

Although there is nothing revolutionary in the idea of working from a location other than the traditional office, ways of working have changed significantly since the early 1990s. Consider that in the early 1990s a typical field engineer might have:

1 Received a print-out of job allocations for the week in the post.
2 Received a phone call the night before detailing job changes.

3 Spent time out on the road with little or no communication to or from the office.

4 Called the office from a landline at home at the end of the day.

5 Written job reports by hand at the end of the day.

6 Sent hand-written paperwork to the office by post or dropped into the office periodically.

Today a field engineer is likely to have the option to:

1 Download job instructions and amendments from a central server onto a hand-held PC or ruggedized laptop.

2 Enter job reports into a hand-held instrument or laptop and upload information back to the central office.

3 Print out job reports onsite and give a copy to customer.

4 Communicate regularly with central office by mobile phone or email.

5 Drop into satellite offices to complete further secretarial duties.

Tools for the mobile worker

As you can see from the previous section, there is an increasing number of tools that can help you to work more flexibly on the move. Some, such as hand-held PCs, are tools that you can carry with you wherever you go. Others, like faxes, will more likely be available in satellite offices or telecentres en route. The most commonly used mobile tools at the present time are the mobile phone, Personal Digital Assistant (PDA) or palmtop, and the laptop. There are several mobile working options open to you:

- To use battery operated hand-held PCs or laptops with or without Internet access.
- To use a phone and laptop to access the Internet.
- To use the facilities of a business centre, telecentre, satellite office, Internet café or similar.
- To connect to the Internet on the move using wireless technologies.

We will look at each of these in a little more detail.

Using hand-held PCs or laptops

Most people buy battery-operated hand-held PCs or laptops with the aim of working more flexibly. Whether the idea is to work on the train or work out of a client office for the day, having a portable PC will increase your chances of being able to work anywhere anytime.

Sharing files

At the very least, portable PCs can be used as stand-alone machines. You can save your work files on to a storage facility (hard disk, CD ROM, memory stick) and access them through the appropriate software stored on your machine.

If you do not have an immediate Internet connection you may have to find some way to share files saved on your PC with colleagues. You can do this by saving files on to a floppy disk, CD ROM or memory stick and then copying them on to another machine. If you think you may eventually have access to the Internet, you could save your files on to the hard disk inside the PC and then when you reach your destination, attach and forward the files via email.

Docking stations

Many companies provide laptops and docking stations for flexible staff. You may also consider a docking station for home use. The idea is that when you are out on the road you have all the advantages of using a portable PC. When you come back into the office you can turn your laptop into a fully operational desktop PC by plugging it into a docking station. A docking station will typically house a full-size screen, full-size keyboard and mouse as well as connections to peripheral devices such as printers, faxes and CD ROM drives.

TIP: If you are going to be travelling with your laptop for some time, make sure that your battery is fully charged before you leave home, and carry the charging unit with you so that you can connect to a power source as soon as is practical. As a precaution, buy a second battery to use in emergencies.

If you are buying a laptop for the first time think carefully about what you need to use it for. For instance, do you just want the flexibility to work in any room in the house or do you want to take your laptop on the road?

You can purchase a laptop off the shelf, in which case it will come ready made with an inbuilt set of tools, or you can choose to have one custom built to your own specification.

Laptops vary in size, weight and functionality, and these characteristics are important considerations for flexible workers. For example, if you don't intend to carry your laptop around very often you may be happy to settle for a slightly heavier one that has a large display screen and built-in storage drives. If, on the other hand, you intend to lug it with you wherever you go, you may prefer to forgo the large screen and built-in storage drives in favour of a lighter model.

Here are some things to consider:

- **Speed** – check out the microprocessor. The higher range Pentium processors are generally found in the more expensive machines.
- **Memory** – make sure your laptop has at least 128MB (Megabytes) of RAM (Random Access Memory). You should realistically expect 256MB in a new laptop and ideally 512MB or above.
- **Hard disk** – as software programs are becoming increasingly memory intensive you should aim to have a hard disk capacity of 20GB (gigabytes) or higher. You would normally expect 40GB or above these days.
- **Storage** – think about how you want to back up your data or share information with others. Do you want to save and read information stored on CD-ROM, floppy disk, DVD or zip disks? Do you need to have more than one of these storage devices? If you opt to have in-built storage devices the laptop may be larger and heavier than if you attach them as external devices as and when you need.
- **Battery life** – if you need to operate on the move for long periods of time check the life of the battery. It may be an option to fit a second battery or carry a charged spare.
- **Screen** – screens vary in size (typically 30–43 cm) and clarity. Active matrix screens produce clearer images. Screens with backlighting make it easier for you to work in poor lighting. However, as you might expect, the clearer the image and larger the screen, generally the higher the price.
- **Printing** – make sure that you have a port to which you can connect a printer. New printers often connect to USB (universal serial bus) ports.

- **Connections** – a lot of devices like web cameras and memory sticks plug into USB ports so it would be a good idea to make sure that you have several USB ports available.
- **Docking** – if you want to connect your laptop to a full-size screen and keyboard when not on the road, check that it can connect to a docking station.
- **Internet access** – if you want to be able to access the Internet with your laptop make sure it has an internal modem fitted.
- **Wireless** – if you think that at some stage in the future you will want to have wireless access to the Internet, go for a laptop with in-built wireless capability. It is also a good idea to purchase a PC with an expansion slot so that you can add a wireless card, a network card or extra memory at some stage.

Accessing the Internet using a phone and laptop

To access the Internet you typically need a modem to convert the digital signals from your PC into signals that can be passed down the telephone line. Providing you have a laptop with an in-built modem, you can connect your laptop to an ordinary phone line and dial up to the Internet from wherever you are. If there is no landline available, you can use your mobile phone as a dial-up modem.

To be able to use your laptop and phone in this way you need:

- A mobile phone that can act as a modem or a PC card that simulates a mobile phone. This slots into the PC card slot on your laptop. However, as this is quite an expensive option most people use the real thing.
- Some means of connecting the two pieces of equipment together. In the early days of mobile phones this would have been done using a cable. Nowadays the two can connect without cables using wireless technology. If you have a laptop and mobile phone that have infra-red ports, they can communicate via infra-red signals. More commonly and more reliably these days, many devices are bluetooth-enabled and communicate with each other via short radio waves. For more information on bluetooth see page 206.
- To install the drivers from the CD ROM that comes with your mobile phone on to your laptop. Drivers are software programs that tell different pieces of equipment how to work with each other. Once you have installed the drivers your

mobile phone will appear as a modem in the control panel settings on your laptop.

- To ask your mobile supplier to allow you to make data calls. Your tariff will be adjusted accordingly.
- To log on to the Internet. You can usually do this by going to dial-up networking options. There you can create an entry with details of phone numbers, log ins, IP addresses and so on, for each modem listed. Choose your mobile phone and connect to the Internet.

PC and Internet facilities

If you are working away from home or want to keep in touch with the office while on holiday there are a growing number of establishments that provide Internet access.

Internet establishments

If you don't want to carry a laptop with you, you can always use the services of an Internet or cyber café. Internet cafés can be found in most city centres around the world as well as in a number of remote locations. If you want to plan ahead and get a list of Internet cafés before you travel, visit www.cybercafes.com. It boasts a database of 4,205 Internet cafés located in 140 countries across the world. Similarly, www.netcafeguide.com and www.cybercaptive.com will give you an extensive choice of global Internet cafés. Cybercaptive currently lists 6,076 cyber cafés, Internet access points and Internet kiosks in 167 countries.

Internet establishments come in all shapes and sizes. Some are large shops filled with rows of computers, others, like libraries or gaming enterprises, may have only a small area dedicated to Internet access. Generally you can walk in off the street and ask to use the Internet. You will be allocated a PC and logged on to the Internet. Although some facilities operate a slot-machine system where you insert money before you begin a session and top it up as required, many are personally managed. In the latter case, the manager will log the time that you use and charge you accordingly.

Before you use a facility you should check out the rates. These can vary substantially, even between competing facilities in the same neighbourhood. However, in big cities the hourly rate is generally low and, unless you are using these types of services extensively, you may find that the difference between facilities is not worth worrying about. It can be quite a different story if you are using more remote facilities; there have been stories of travellers stung for Internet access on remote islands where connections to the Internet can be much more costly.

Internet terminals and kiosks

You can also access the Internet from terminals in key public places like airports or from a growing number of Internet kiosks. These work on a similar basis to Internet cafés, although occasionally you may find a facility that is available to use free of charge. For example, in Singapore airport there are free Internet terminals in arrivals and departure lounges.

Case study: E-payphones

In the UK, BT plans to install 20,000 blue e-payphones nationwide over the next few years, the majority of which will provide a high-speed broadband connection to the Internet. You can use these kiosks to make standard telephone calls, send and pick up emails and send text messages to mobile phones. Each has a touch-sensitive screen that you can use to browse up-to-the-minute news, sports and weather bulletins. You can also get information on your locality such as places to shop and eat.

Self check

Things to watch out for

If you are using the Internet in a public place you can never be sure that the information you are sending or receiving is secure. As a rule of thumb you should not make financial transactions online nor divulge private or confidential information.

Make sure that you don't

- Bank online. ❏
- Shop online. ❏
- Give out personal information. ❏

Make sure that you do

- Log out of your email account when you have finished. ❏

If you use a web-based email program it is not uncommon to find that when you log on you can see someone else's account.

In addition to security issues there are other drawbacks. Many public systems will prevent you from downloading attachments. So, if you are relying on receiving information by attachment you may have to make alternative arrangements.

Telecentres and business centres

A growing number of centres have been set up around the country to provide you with high-speed access to the Internet and business facilities. Centres come in different guises. Some have been set up with the express purpose of serving the needs of the local community, others have a more commercial focus. The purpose of the community-based telecentres is typically three-fold:

1 To attract location-independent or global work to the region.
2 To provide skills development through access to learning materials and new technologies.
3 To provide a support network for the local community.

Case study: Telecentres

West Lothian telecentre in Scotland (32 km west of Edinburgh) was set up as part of a vocational training project for unemployed adults and women returners. The centre now provides general business services to the public.

The Brampton telecentre, managed by Carlisle City Council's Economic Development Unit in the UK, is situated in a rural market town near Carlisle. It provides IT and business access to the public.

At the very least, working from such centres will give you the opportunity to escape from the house and mix with other people in a similar situation. Perhaps most importantly, many of them also give you the chance to meet clients in prestigious office surroundings, as well as having the use of meeting rooms, video conferencing facilities and a range of IT and secretarial services. They are similar in principle to traditional serviced offices but with an accent on space, technology and Internet access. To find a telecentre in your area, use a search engine to search for 'telecentre' or consult your local business advisory centres.

Case study: Macmerry

If you live in East Lothian in Scotland, you can work out of what is thought to be the UK's first satellite park, located in Macmerry. It is estimated that somewhere around 45% of the population of Macmerry commute into Edinburgh, and it is hoped that the facilities provided on the park will encourage people to work locally instead of travelling to work. The man behind the idea, David Fyffe, already has plans to roll out the scheme nationwide over the next 12 months.

If you are looking for a business centre to call your temporary home, visit www.regus.com. Regus offers fully-equipped offices in 330 cities and 55 countries. The company provides a range of services that includes voice, mail and fax handling. You may be particularly interested in the Regus virtual office, which allows you to use a Regus address as your business address without you ever having to be there. Regus staff answer the phone in your business name or forward your mail and messages to designated addresses. This service entitles you to use Regus lounges, cyber cafés, secretarial services and 2 hours of office space usage per week at any of the 700 locations worldwide. You can also book additional office or meeting space on a 'pay as you need' basis.

In addition to commercial business centres, many private organizations operate their own satellite or touchdown centres. These typically provide facilities for employees to drop in on an ad hoc basis and use a PC, phone, desk and sometimes secretarial services. Recent improvements in remote access security have led many companies to take a more flexible approach to remote working; it is probably worth asking whether or not such facilities exist.

Case study: Scottish Enterprise

The mission of Scottish Enterprise in the UK is to help the people and businesses of Scotland to succeed. As a forward-thinking economic development agency, its headquarters at Atlantic Quay, Glasgow are an outstanding showcase for flexible working. At any time on a given day, staff can choose to work in a way that suits their business and individual needs. For example, they can meet people for a chat in an informal breakout area or head for a hot office if they need to work in peace and quiet. Work-space options include:

- **Touchdown areas** – short-stay areas where staff can plug in a laptop and log on to the Scottish Enterprise computer network, check emails and make telephone calls. These areas operate on a first-come, first-served basis.
- **Hot desks** – for people who need to book a desk for a few hours or a day at a time.
- **Carrels** – bookable study booths for staff who want to work in a quiet area.
- **Hot offices** – small offices that can be used for concentrated quiet PC work, reading or writing.
- **Project areas** – semi-enclosed areas located away from normal desks. Primarily used for ad hoc meetings and brainstorming sessions, they are equipped with flexible furniture and whiteboards.
- **Informal meeting spaces** – coffee areas and seating spaces.
- **Oasis areas** – each of the main office floors also has an oasis area. These are semi-enclosed areas with access to shared printers, faxes and photocopiers. You can pick up mail and catch up on the latest noticeboard news while you get a drink from a vending machine.

There is a team of people available to help staff and visitors to book work spaces, and provide ongoing support and advice about computers, equipment and other facilities. Staff are also able to book the service they want online.

Wireless communication

If you want a greater degree of flexibility over where you work, either in the home or out and about, then you should look at the range of wireless-enabled equipment currently on the market. Wireless equipment allows you to connect to the Internet without using cables. As the number of wireless areas that you can use to connect to the Internet (known as 'wireless hotspots') is set to grow exponentially, wireless access to the Internet will be more readily available for mobile workers and travellers. Wireless technologies transmit information long distance through the air on radio waves.

How does wireless information get transmitted?
The wireless device that you are using, such as a PDA, mobile phone or laptop, creates information which is then attached to a carrier wave by a device called a modulator. Sometimes the

modulator is built into the device, as in the case of a hand-held computer. Sometimes the modulator is housed elsewhere, as in the case of a modulator that converts TV signals into a form that can be carried by radio frequency (RF) waves. The information is then sent along the wave with the help of a transmitter. When it reaches its destination a demodulator transforms the information back into signals that can be read by the receiving device.

Wireless standards

Although the principle of wireless communication is simple, the ways in which individual devices send and receive information using RF is a little more complicated. A TV signal will be created, modulated, transmitted and demodulated in a different way from voice data generated by a telephone.

The fact that there are many different wireless devices (including laptops, PDAs, mobile phones, and headsets) on the market creates a headache for hardware and software manufacturers who need to find ways to make devices talk to each other. Although there have been significant developments in wireless technology, there is still some way to go before we can operate seamlessly anytime and anywhere! One of the key issues is that there is no one standard which defines how different wireless devices communicate with each other and the Internet. Two of the main standards available at the moment are Bluetooth and IEEE 802.11.

Bluetooth

Bluetooth is named after Harald Blatand, a Viking King who united Denmark in the 900s. Like Blatand (translated as 'Bluetooth'), bluetooth uses technology to 'unite' or connect a range of different devices.

Bluetooth is hailed as the next generation of mobile technology. Bluetooth wireless devices work on a short-range radio frequency and are able to recognize and talk to each other without the need for cables. You can buy bluetooth-enabled devices for all manner of home entertainment and PC systems. You can get bluetooth-enabled hi-fis, TVs, mobile phones, laptops, headsets and printers.

Just as the infra-red zapper once impressed with its ability to control the TV from the sofa, a bluetooth headset can automatically switch from playing music to receiving an incoming call on your mobile phone. Similarly, a bluetooth laptop can connect to a mobile phone and send emails while you are on the move. It is possible to have a wireless earpiece for your mobile – you can be up to 9m away from your mobile phone and it will still pick up calls.

How does a bluetooth device work?

Each device contains an in-built chip that enables it to operate as a short-range digital radio, sending and receiving information to and from compatible devices within its range. All you have to do is switch it on and wait while it searches for other devices. There is no need for you to install it or tell it which other pieces of equipment to search for. It automatically 'knows' what to do. A bluetooth machine will store the 'profiles' of devices that it can communicate with as well as instructions on how information should be sent between them.

Should I consider buying bluetooth devices?

The main benefits of using bluetooth technology are that:

- The devices are wireless and so there is no need to carry or set up cables.
- The devices are self-operating and you don't need to have any special skills to set them up.

Bluetooth is one option for getting compatible devices to talk to each other. However, bluetooth wireless devices are generally aimed at the home user and cater particularly well in the field of home entertainment. With the range of pressures placed on today's flexible worker, you may prefer to go for devices that work with the wireless network standard known as IEEE 802.11. Among other things you can link lots of PCs together and share resources such as scanners, printers, storage devices and Internet access. You can also access information stored on a private company network.

IEEE 802.11 wireless standard

Bluetooth devices establish a direct wireless connection to each other (known as a peer-to-peer network), whereas an IEEE 802.11 wireless network device will generally connect to an access point rather than another device. The access point serves as a bridge between your PC and a company network or between your PC and the Internet. You can buy an access point for the home, connect it to your modem and theoretically be up and running with a wireless network in no time.

An access point is made up of:

- a radio transmitter
- a radio receiver
- an interface to a wired network.

For a computer to communicate with a wider network via the access point you must make sure that it is fitted with an 802.11 compatible wireless network card. If the software is set up to load as part of the start-up sequence, when you switch your computer on it will search for the access point. If it receives signals from several access points, it will choose one based on strength of signal and the least number of errors.

IEEE 802.11 network cards can also be used to establish a wireless connection between computers in a peer-to-peer network so that files and printers can be shared without going through a wireless access point.

Wireless access to the Internet at home

Many flexible workers are fast installing wi-fi (wireless fidelity) networks in their homes so that other members of the family can share files and get rapid access to the Internet from different rooms. Microsoft Windows XP works well with wi-fi networks and many Macintosh machines come with in-built capability.

If you are keen to work from a variety of locations, including different areas of the house, you will need one of the following:

- A laptop that has certified wi-fi capability built in. If you already have a laptop that does not have wireless capability, you may be able to upgrade your laptop capability by purchasing a wi-fi PCMCIA card.
- A wireless-enabled PDA. Again if your PDA does not currently have wireless capability, you may need to buy an add-in card.
- If you want to use wireless access at home, you may also need to buy the equipment to create a wireless access point depending on the technological requirements dictated by your current system.

Case study: Mark

Mark is a consultant who works from home. For the most part he works from an office set up in an upstairs bedroom but occasionally in the evening he takes his paperwork downstairs and works from the lounge. Recently he invested in a wireless-enabled laptop.

'It occurred to me that I was pretty limited in the kinds of work that I could do in other parts of the house. I could only really read paperwork or write reports by hand. Then a few months ago I saw an advert for a wireless laptop and I decided to invest in one. I'm not particularly techie so I asked a friend to set it up for me. I was surprised. The set-up seemed quite straightforward. The first day that I used it I sat in the garden sun lounger and logged on to the net. I couldn't believe it! It was fantastic. The signal strength was strong and I spent a good few hours surfing for information. Since then I've tried it out in the lounge and kitchen. The signal strength differs slightly depending on which part of the house I am. It seems to work best when it's directly underneath the wireless access point in my office. I have to say though that it's been a brilliant investment. As well as giving me flexibility to move around, my children now use it to do their homework on the Internet while I'm using the Internet on the other PC.'

There are many providers of wireless equipment and it pays to shop around. Search the net for 'wireless network providers'.

Wireless on the move

The ideal for a flexible worker is to reach a stage where you can be completely location-independent. But just how do you access the Internet on the move? The answer is to find yourself a wireless hotspot – a location that has a wireless access point that you can hook into.

Wireless hotspots are the latest rage in broadband services. Telecomms companies are installing wireless access points across the country in a range of public places such as restaurants, hotels, service stations, airports and train stations. The idea is that you can take your laptop to one of these points, connect to it and log on to the Internet at broadband speeds. All you have to do is:

- use your laptop to search for a list of available networks
- select an appropriate connection
- type in your wireless code, and away you go.

For a list of wi-fi hotspot locations try www.wifi411.com/networks or www.hotspot-locations.com. Select a country, state and city to see a list of locations.

It is estimated that by 2006 there will be 135,000 hotspots worldwide, and that by 2007 there will be in excess of 30,000 hotspots installed across Europe alone. Given these figures, a time may come when you can connect to wireless hotspots along the full length of your journey irrespective of whether you are travelling in the UK or abroad. For example, you can already catch an intercity train from York to London and pick up your emails and work files on the way. You can meet a client for lunch in Starbucks and use your laptop to demonstrate online products. And, finally, you can sit down in your hotel lounge at the end of a hard day, hook into a wireless hotspot and catch up with fluctuations in the stock market.

Case study: GNER

GNER is enjoying great success as the first UK rail operator to offer wireless Internet access on board its trains. The service, which provides uninterrupted Internet access at speeds of up to 125 miles per hour, was trialled earlier this year. Now, in what appears to be the largest project of its kind in the world, GNER are looking to equip all 302 trains in their 'Mallard' fleet with wireless Internet capability.

The wi-fi service will be available to all passengers with a wi-fi enabled laptop equipped with a wireless Internet card, making travelling time more productive for both the business traveller and those on a pleasure trip. Customers will be able to pick up and send emails, surf the web, shop and bank online, access the latest travel information and use Virtual Private Networks (VPNs) to access company information on the move.

Standard-class passengers log on, pay a small fee by credit card (based on the length of time to be spent online) and are then given an Internet access code. First-class passengers have access to the service included in the ticket price. Trains offering wireless Internet are clearly marked with window stickers and notices explaining how to take advantage of the system. Information is also provided on the departure boards at some stations such as Kings Cross.

According to figures published by Icomera, the take-up of the service is proving to be incredibly popular. The growth rate across all passengers is thought to be 77% per week and among first-class passengers it appears to be more than doubling each week. From its own research, GNER has elicited some commercially interesting information: 67% of first-class passengers said that they were keen to use the service again; 88% said that they would recommend it to colleagues; and 25% said that they would choose to travel more frequently with GNER if the service was offered on all trains. In addition, 2.5% of standard-class users have upgraded to first-class tickets.

GNER spokesman John Gelson says, 'Wireless Internet is already proving invaluable to our business customers as a means of transforming train time into more productive working time. The technology also has major potential to create a more enjoyable leisure time experience on our trains, and that's one of the major reasons why we're now making it available throughout our new look trains.'

Further details of the service, as well as hints and tips on making the most of wi-fi on the move, can be found on www.gnermobileoffice.co.uk.

Payment options

So if you are keen to give it a go, how and what do you pay for these hotspot services? The answer depends to some degree on how often you anticipate using the service of a particular provider, and your location at the time. Some companies operate a voucher system that allows you to pay for hotspot access on an hourly, daily or monthly basis or gives you the option of taking out a contract for a longer period of time.

Are hotspots all that they are cracked up to be?

Using a wireless hotspot sounds great in principle, but how straightforward is it? The truth of the matter is that these schemes are still in their infancy and there are some practical issues that need to be resolved before mobile workers will feel confident using them.

One of the biggest drawbacks is that as you travel around, you are likely to move between hotspot zones that are serviced by different suppliers, and at the moment there are few standard ways of connecting to each. This means that as you enter a new zone you may have to register with the individual supplier, arrange payment and adjust your laptop network settings to make them compatible. Perhaps not a prospect for the faint-hearted!

In addition to these limitations, wireless connections are also weaker the further away you get from an access point, and speed may be an issue if lots of users are downloading large complex files at the same time. However, companies are busy developing systems that will allow you to connect seamlessly and effortlessly to different wireless networks irrespective of who your service supplier is. In the future you will also be able to look forward to receiving one bill irrespective of which wireless network you have been using.

Summary

Recent technological innovations have undoubtedly taken the concept of flexible working to new heights. The arrival of the Internet followed by wireless technologies has meant that you can now pretty much work anytime anywhere. You can call the office on your mobile while standing on a station platform, access the Internet from a wireless hotspot on the train, and work on secure company files from your hotel room.

index